A CANADIAN

Conversations with Time
Peter Harcourt

JOURNEY

This book was written and published with the assistance of the Canada Council, the Ontario Arts Council and others. Edited with the assistance of the Ontario Publishing Centre of the Ministry of Culture and Communications.

ISBN 0 88750 983 5 (hardcover)
ISBN 0 88750 984 3 (softcover)

Cover: the author at the age of five with his father, John, his grandmother, Elizabeth and his sister, Barbara
Book design by Michael Macklem
Edited by David Helwig

Printed in Canada

PUBLISHED IN CANADA BY OBERON PRESS

For Joy, who always said I should tell my story;
and for David, who asked me to.

One

"Autobiography begins with a sense of being alone. It is an orphan form."—John Berger.

"Memory is the purgative by which we rid ourselves of the present. Memory is a form of hope."—Timothy Findley.

The past is a darkness. Memory is opaque. Yet from the outset, I knew I was living in a space out of time. Cultural schizophrenia is a legacy of modernity and this inheritance was bestowed upon me as a birthright.

As we all now know, the western world has produced a culture of patriarchy. Indeed, I grew up in a culture of war. But there was a difference. Since all able men were away from home, I was surrounded by women. Even before the war, my father was kept apart from us.

I was constantly shuffled off to the nursery with my sister, Barbara, so as not to disturb my father. There, because my sister was older and I adored her, we played girls' games. We played with Jane Arden cut-outs. I kept pleading with her: "Can't we play war games?" "No," she said. "If there's ever a real war, then we'll play war games." In 1939 when war broke out, triumphantly I accosted my indifferent sister: "Now we can play war games!" We played Jane Arden goes to war.

We did everything together, Barbara and I. I thought she was wonderful. She was loved by everyone and celebrated by all our relatives. I am not sure she even liked me. She simply had to endure me. After all, I was male—at least latently. The rest of the world was female and the women all got on with one another.

Except for Nellie. Nellie was the live-in maid. She was never called a nanny. That would have given her too much respect. She did the cooking and the cleaning and had to deal

3

with my sister and me. She loved me and I loved her back. But we were outcasts. My mother couldn't stand her. Perhaps she feared that Nellie and I were too close. Perhaps we were. I don't remember. But if there is any memory of affection during those early years growing up on College Street in Toronto in the nineteen-thirties, it is a memory of Nellie. I have no affective memory of my parents at all.

However, I don't want to write about my family. I want to write about the space in which I lived.

It was a fenced-in space, a sealed-off space—a prison space really. The prison was designed less to keep things in than to keep them out; and what it kept out were the multiple realities of the rest of the world. Meanwhile, we were also kept in— especially me, the burgeoning male.

I had been a sickly child. Or so I was told. I was not strong enough to go out on the street and play with other boys. Or so I was told. Actually, as I gradually began to realize, out on the street were working-class kids and worse than that, Jewish kids. Since the Harcourts had always gone to Ridley College, or so I was told, I had to be careful in choosing my friends. I was not at all like other boys. I was superior. Or so I was told. Meanwhile my parents sent me to Dewson Street public school.

I wasn't allowed to play with Paul, the barber's son, who lived across the street. Although he wasn't Jewish, he was inferior in some other way. Perhaps because his parents hadn't been to Ridley College. Possibly because he could throw and catch a ball far better than I and could certainly run faster when, in the schoolyard, we played tag or baseball. I couldn't understand. Different, I recognized. But inferior?

In those days of strict educational principles, we were all arranged in class according to academic rank. The kid with the best marks sat on the right-hand side of the teacher in the front row. The class dunce sat on the left at the back. We all knew where we stood—especially when we sat. On Jewish holidays, the front two rows were empty. On the first occupied seats was a girl or two and then there was me. Was I allowed to play with girls? I imagine peer pressure forbade it. I remember walking home alone each day after school. I had to get my rest. Or so I was told. I had to be resealed within the space of my confinement—with my sister and Nellie.

In spite of these insulations, I did acquire one or two friends. My best friend, Milton, was Ukrainian but that was okay. In any case, by that time, my father was away at war. Once Grade 8 had been suffered through, Dewson Street public school split neatly along a racial divide: the Jewish kids went to Harbord and the gentiles to Bloor. It was as simple as that. At that time in that district, yellow or black kids didn't seem to go to school at all.

During our first day at Bloor, we trundled into the school auditorium and were told that we would be assigned to our classes not on the basis of merit but of name. Not excellence but alphabet would determine our fate. There was one exception. The kids who wanted to play in the band would be put in the same class. Terrified of losing one another, Milton and I both claimed to be musical so that we could stay together. From this desperate fear of loneliness, my musical life began.

I had had a longing for music before this event. My sister had taken piano lessons. I was fascinated with the process, with all the singing and counting, and I pleaded with my mother to let me have lessons. I was firmly refused. Music was for girls. Boys were intended for finer things.

Throughout these early years there is so little I remember; but I know my culture imposed upon me a life of denials— apparently even the right to imagine. Like music, imagination was for girls.

Once in Grade 9 at Bloor Collegiate in a wood-working class I was roundly chastised by my teacher. He was old and dour but seemed centred in himself and could make things, invent things, even though he was male. He turned on me one day for humming while I worked. "You're acting like an old woman," he admonished. I felt thoroughly humiliated. In any case, I wasn't allowed to continue shop beyond the first year because shop was for the regular guys and, apparently, I was already deemed an intellectual. It is so strange: I had no idea of the forces that were working upon me.

Certainly, from those early days of Jane Arden, I grew up within the imaginative world created by my sister. She choreographed all the games we played; and in the early years, we were always together.

Especially during summer. In July, before my father went to war, we spent time in Muskoka; but in August, we were shipped off to the family farm near Cayuga in the Niagara peninsula. This place provided the experiences that have remained in my memory, that have played a major role in determining my sense of self.

These August summers are like scenes from a film by Ingmar Bergman. Everything was elegant, spacious, ritualized and repressed. A low-church puritanism afflicted everything we did, everything we said.

The farm was called the Hermitage. It was the ancestral home of my father's mother's family. The Davis family. Once you turned off the main road about a mile before Cayuga, you reached the house by turning right along a country lane that passed through a wooded lot. To my young eyes, it was a forest. Driving along this wooded avenue never ceased to thrill me. Indeed, it thrilled me still in 1969 when, with my marriage breaking up, I took my children on a pilgrimage to my past so that they might know a bit about me. Of course, they didn't care. They were too young. It meant nothing to them. But it meant a lot to me.

Entering that space was like entering a fairytale. It was like returning to a different period of time. I also knew that, because of the isolation of this wonderful family farm, I would be alone with my sister. I anticipated the thrill of impending transgression. In such an atmosphere of puritanical repression where everything was either obligatory or forbidden, I knew that I would experience a sense of sin.

The house was an elegant example of southern Ontario architecture. Built in red brick with lace-like wooden trim, it revealed the scars of disjunctive additions. It was full of irregularities. There was scarcely a level floor in the house; and the spacious kitchen that had initially been a shed was heated even in summer by a large wood-burning stove. On that magnificent black structure all the meals were prepared and within it the angel cake was baked by Aunt Margaret in celebration of our annual arrival.

Margaret was the most loving of the women at the Hermitage. It was her house, in fact. She was the youngest of a family of five. Margaret had stayed in it after her sisters had married and moved away. She stayed to look after her father, refusing to marry until—as they said in those days—he had passed away. Fred Goodwillie, a lawyer initially from the west, had waited for her for over twenty years. Or so I was told. She was 40 by the time she got married. And by the time Uncle Fred was allowed to move in, all the other sisters, their husbands having died, were moving back.

Fred and Margaret probably never had any private time together. They certainly had no time together when Barbara and I were there. They were surrounded by the Davis sisters. There was Helen, and Annie, and another aunt in town. It was a bit like *Cries & Whispers*. There was also Uncle Ed in Cayuga. He wore thick glasses. But the men were distinctly marginal to this women's estate.

Fred Goodwillie was, in fact, a figure of fun. A fastidious man, a humourless man, undoubtedly a lonely man, Uncle Fred was the butt of innumerable jokes. The women were always mocking him behind his back, thereby undermining any dignity he might have had.

"Who's been throwing peach skins on Auntie's clean steps?" he bellowed out one afternoon when Aunt Helen, my sister and I were eating peaches in the sun. Like an on-going gag from the Jack Benny show, this angry outburst became a recurring joke that used to throw us into fits of laughter for years to come. Of course, there was nothing funny about it. What became a hilarious joke between Aunt Helen and my sister was the spectacle of a man attempting to assert his authority in this matriarchal space to which he didn't belong.

I cannot see myself in any of these scenes. I cannot imagine what I must have felt. Nor can I remember anything I might have said. I took my cue from the women. I laughed whenever it was appropriate to laugh; but to this day, when I lose my temper, I find the spectacle of male authority attempting to assert itself risible in the extreme.

War was raging in Europe, and Uncle Fred spent hours in his study, listening to news on the radio and moving coloured pins about a huge map on the wall. Except for the traditional noon-time dinner each Sunday, he took all his meals there. It was a sealed off space. The world of men. A veteran of the First World War, he followed all the battles with the attention of a general. Sometimes when he was out, I would venture into this world of maps and books and leather to inhale the smells of masculinity. But I was never invited by Fred himself. I was not yet accepted as male.

The Hermitage was a wonderful piece of land. Initially 60 acres in size, it was flanked on one side by this marvellous stretch of wood in which all sorts of shrubs and trees crowded together in mysterious dialogue, and on the other by the Grand River, with its stately if even then polluted path toward Lake Erie. To the west was a vineyard and down from it the vegetable garden where all the food was grown that we ate when we were there in the summer and which we helped Aunt Margaret to bottle up as preserves for the winter to come.

Further down toward the river were the flats in which the

cattle grazed. There were five cows, of course all of them female, and one lonely horse, appropriately male.

There was Ruby, the herd mother—a ruby-red Guernsey who must have produced thousands of gallons of milk in her day. When she trudged up the lane every evening to be milked, her teats virtually dragged upon the ground. She was gentle and (I want to say) loving. She was Buddhist in her view of life and accepted everything that happened to her. She always seemed to recognize us as if we were friends.

There was also Sylvia, the high-strung Jersey, who provided the richest milk with the thickest cream. She mistrusted everything. She greeted everyone with hostility, her head lowered, her horns ready, her eyes alert and fearful, as if we were going to take something from her, which, of course, we were. And there were others—a Holstein, another Guernsey and many progeny of Ruby but of mixed breed. And there was Gus, the solitary horse.

During our walks in the evening we, Aunt Margaret, my sister and I, would sing songs about Gus, about his imagined loneliness. I think we even acknowledged his sexual isolation. "Oh, you can't marry five pretty cows," we'd conclude, all a-giggle. It was appropriate. Even the animals formed a matriarchy, isolating the single male.

Between the house and the beginnings of the farm-land itself was a wonderful stretch of lawn marked by two magnificent oaks. Beneath these oaks was a grass so fine that I used to marvel at its beauty. I have never experienced grass like that again. Over toward the vineyard, there was an apple tree shaped as if deliberately for us to climb in it, beneath which was a vast spread of lily of the valley.

I had no idea how all these things had come to be. The thought of someone having planted them, having designed them at some far-off time, never occurred to me. Everything was simply there, as we would cry out in church every Sunday morning, as manifestation of the glorious bounty of God.

9

Trees have played an ennobling role in my life. Those two oaks at the end of the Hermitage lawn were matched by two huge elms at the end of our garden on College Street. I don't know how young I was when I first began to stand by these twin sets of trees trying to be tall like them, dignified and serene. Much later, when in England and in distress at the difficulties of the first months of my marriage, I would flee our little flat in Kentish Town, strike out across wonderful Hampstead Heath and find yet another set of trees in the estate in Kenwood toward the north end of the heath. These were beech trees, tall and silver; and especially in the winter when free from leaves, they would stretch upward into the sunless sky as if toward something finer than this miserable life on earth. I wanted to do the same. I wanted to rise above my own insecurities, my petty, uncertain demands and our shared sense of failure. I wanted to be quiet, strong, accepting and enduring—like a tree.

If during the early years of my life, my existence in Toronto was like a prison sealed off from the realities of the world, my August sojourns at the Hermitage were like a pastoral reprieve. They provided an escape from those urban deprivations, even if, ultimately, the Hermitage was also a prison equally shut off from the realities of the rural world.

I can scarcely remember what I did or felt; but I do remember moments—as from a film viewed long ago, only the flavour of which remains.

At the Hermitage there was also a munificent horse-chestnut tree. It sat on one of the upper lawns with a powerful horizontal branch from which was suspended an intricately fabricated hammock. It had been crocheted. Or so I was told. When not with my sister playing the imaginary games devised by her on another one of the lawns, I would lie in this hammock and contemplate the infinite richness of the branches above me with their already burgeoning fruit. I would imagine myself

Tarzan, swinging from branch to branch, saving from some unspecified distress an unimaginable damsel that required my care.

Somewhere inside me, I still see myself in this way. Surely someone who is anatomically male must save sensitive females from the fate that awaits them in a world of Fred Goodwillies! Surely, if that could be my mission in life, then I might earn the admiration of the women who surrounded me—indeed, engulfed me might be the more appropriate term. Perhaps even my sister would then truly value me, instead of just accepting me as one of life's duties—like a brother or a pet.

When we both were tiny, we slept together—in a large room at the front of the house from which I could look out on those mighty oaks and from which, on a moonlit night, I could see the sky's reflection in the mysterious Grand River. I remember there was great gaiety on the part of my sister when a bolster was ceremoniously deposited in the middle of the bed to keep us from cuddling—not that I remember any cuddles. Quite the opposite. I remember changing our clothes, especially after swimming, and Barbara laughing hilariously at this strange appendage that would look incredibly shrivelled or misaligned in some way. I felt embarrassment at these moments, perhaps a sense of shame—but also an awkward pride that I could provide my sister with laughter in this way.

Those scenes were nothing compared to the merriment we shared at Uncle Fred's matudinal visits to us from time to time. There was something that made his nightshirt stick out in a way I couldn't understand. He would stand on my sister's side of the bed and talk to her about anything. Aunt Margaret caught him with us one morning and peremptorily chased him away. "Fred Goodwillie, you ought to be ashamed of yourself," she cried out in fury. I didn't know why. Perhaps she thought he had wakened us up.

Uncle Fred used to read to my sister in the evenings, sitting on a sofa together in the drawing-room. I don't know what he was reading but I know, as if it had been me, that he loved to fondle the top of her thighs as he read, as during the days he took great pains at teaching her how to hold the teat of a cow in order to milk it—far more pains than he ever took with me.

As I dig down into these scraps of memories what I find most strange is that there was no sense at the time of sexual harassment. These incidents were all part of the general glee with which Uncle Fred was perceived by the women who surrounded him—though perhaps not by his wife. Everything he did seemed further to devalue him. Did Barbara share these tales with our aunts or only with me? I cannot remember. But I know that, collectively, they etched a picture of the pathetic stupidity of the male.

There are also other stories—stories involving women. There is one I remember, obviously told to me by my sister, that is so vivid that it has entered my imagination as if it were my own.

This story involves Aunt Helen. When younger, she had lived in Hamilton where her husband had been a clergyman. When he died, she moved back to the Hermitage, bringing some of her furniture with her. Even then I was impressed by the dining-room chairs. With wicker seats, they were made of oak but with a clover design carved in the back of them in the form of a cross. These chairs seemed to confirm the holiness of her life. I still have that feeling about them because, as I write, they sit downstairs in all their stately antiquity, with their sense of a sanctified past.

However, one night—or so I remember—Helen came into Barbara's room, her doublet all unlaced, her withered dug in her hand, declaiming with great concern: "My paps, which have never given suck, are as hard as rocks." I cannot recall my sister's reply.

Life at the Hermitage was, indeed, full of transgression. It was charged with adult mysteries, with anguish inadequately dealt with, and with pain yet to come. The most traumatic moment concerns, again, my sister. The bolster in the bed between us I couldn't understand but could endure—especially since she made such a joke of it, as she did of everything in those days.

The following year, however, Barbara was assigned her own room. We could no longer sleep together. Was I eight and she ten? Was I ten and she twelve? The decision probably had to do with the presence of blood. My sister had tried to tell me about these female mysteries and I remember my mother talking about the "curse." But I had no way of visualizing any of these secrets. I felt it was my fault. Either it was my fault that my sister was bleeding or perhaps I was becoming like Fred Goodwillie—a masculine figure of fun.

I was terrified sleeping in the big front room that first night on my own. All the floor-boards creaked and the much beloved old house was full of unfamiliar anxieties. I was so distressed, perhaps in ways not at all clear to me, that I wet the bed—something I hadn't done in years.

What an embarrassment! My interior protest against separation! If my sister could leak, surely I too could leak. But were the grief not enough to rankle my spirit for the rest of my life, my aunts—whether practically or sadistically—put the soiled mattress out of the window on the roof of the front porch to dry in the sun. All the neighbours could share in my humiliation. Everyone in Cayuga would know what had occurred. All the way to Dunnville everybody would know that I was not yet a man because I had peed in my bed like a baby.

No wonder I was no longer worthy of sleeping with my sister. In a sense, I have never fully recovered from the shame of that event.

There was another Davis sister that I haven't yet mentioned. She disappeared early but was a dominating presence while she was there. Her name was Elizabeth. She was my father's mother and she was a saint. Or so I was told.

If Margaret was the youngest, Elizabeth was the eldest. She was also the most severe. My memories of her are dim though my feelings remain strong.

My mother told tales of her tyrannical Christianity. Her husband had died when my father was two and she spent the winters with us in Toronto. In the very early days, back in the 1920s, when my parents went out in the evenings, no doubt dancing and drinking and doing the things one did at that time, Grandmother Elizabeth would wait up until well into the morning to have prayers with them before they went to bed. To forgive them their sins.

One afternoon in August at the Hermitage, my sister and I were playing on a swing that Uncle Fred had strung from an over-hanging branch of one of the large oak trees in front of the house. We must have been five and seven at that time, at most. It was my turn to push and I was thrusting my sister higher and higher, creating louder and louder screams that I should stop. Thrilled by my sense of power through my ability to cause terror, I continued to push. Ever higher and higher. My grandmother was sitting with Aunt Margaret on the porch. Little did I care about the fierce exhortations that came from the house. I continued to push, taking delight in the fact that my sister continued to scream.

Was this my first experience of masculine domination? Was it supposed to be my last? The next thing I knew, an angry Aunt Margaret had me by the ear and was dragging me back to the porch to be thoroughly chastised by Saint Elizabeth and sent into the house. Was I locked in a dark closet for hours with no supper? This memory has fused completely with recollections of Ingmar Bergman films; but I do know that later on in the 1950s when I began to see those Swedish films, although they were in a foreign language with English sub-titles, for me, in the excited shock of recognition, they in no way *felt* like foreign films.

What I most remember about Elizabeth was the moment of her death. This moment took forever. Or so it seemed.

The year was 1937. I was six. I can be sure of this because that was the year my younger sister was born. No doubt out of tribute, she too was named Elizabeth although she was always called Sparrow. In a very real way, however, within my family, young Sparrow was not allowed to exist. As a baby, her natural cries and screams at life were locked away somewhere in our large house on College Street, locked away from my grandmother so as not to disturb her final days. In ways that even now I do not understand, my younger sister was invisible. She plays no part in any early memory that I can reach. I know that occasionally she was in Muskoka with us but I cannot remember anything we did together. She never seemed to be in Brockville, a place where we went in July during the war. She certainly never came to the Hermitage.

But where did she go? I don't know. She has been banished from my consciousness just as eventually she later banished herself from what was left of our family. She now lives in Florida and we see one another, almost like strangers, every two or three years. The older I get, however, the more I miss her absent memory.

For years, I knew my grandmother was a saint, no matter how tyrannical, but never more so than the day she died. When I was ushered into her room to offer an obligatory goodbye kiss, I saw her aura. It was green and purple—green around her head and purple as it radiated out into the room. I can still see it today. The pale nimbi I knew from the calendar pictures of saintly Christians were nothing compared to this radiant multi-coloured glow. Being in that room on that final day, I knew that I was in the presence of something terrifying. Indeed, I was.

She was buried in an Anglican church near Cayuga. As we sang our way through all twelve verses of "Abide With Me," I

15

thought I would die from weeping. But what was I weeping about, really? Certainly not at the loss of an enriching human love. Perhaps mostly at the recognition of mortality, at the sadistic ceremony of an Anglican death. Fast flows the eventide. Probably I was also weeping at the sense of my own sinfulness. Surely, with such an unworthy little boy, with such a transgressor of the world's expectations, no Lord would ever with me abide.

These rural memories are the most vivid of my early years. And yet, beyond the wooded shelter of the entrance to the Hermitage, lay an entire world that I was not allowed to see. No one ever talked about it, except in terms of caution. It was as if nothing of value could exist outside the decaying garrison of my family.

At harvest time, all kinds of unfamiliar people would arrive on the scene, including young boys about the same age as I. They were all farmers—local kids. I was not allowed to play with them. While sometimes Uncle Fred would assign me a job—a play job, really, not a proper job such as the other boys had—I knew that my real place was in the kitchen, working with Aunt Margaret, peeling potatoes for the men.

I had no way of dealing with these events. No words. No concepts. I didn't know about the class system. I just knew that fraternization outside the family was always disallowed. It was not until much later when fate propelled me to England to study literature at Cambridge that I began to understand the world in which I had been confined. It was not until I read Jane Austen, particularly *Mansfield Park*, that I understood the mind-set of those guardians who had tried to keep me apart from the contemporary world. Obviously, I was a "gentleman"—or at least supposed to be. But since there were no other gentlemen in the world in which I was placed—certainly not at Etobicoke High School where I finally went to school—my early years were lived within an extraordinary solitude.

My teenage years are not quite so shrouded by the repressions of memory. Like many teenage years, however, they were immersed in triviality.

It was some time after the war before my father came home. He had commanded a medical field unit with General Montgomery's Eighth Army in Italy and there was some dishonour associated with his discharge. I still don't know about this. In any case, he came home in a rage.

"God-damned Krauts and Wops! Who the hell won the war?" Even then I regretted his intolerance but understood his position. My father had fought in two world wars—that the world might be free, as he would have formulated it. To maintain angloceltic male authority, is how we might formulate it today.

My father was intellectually an extremely simple man. He read no books. He saw no films. I believe he was a compassionate doctor. Whether he was a good doctor, I have no way of knowing. By the time he returned to our house on College Street, the entire district was full of Italians and Germans— especially Germans who, liberated from the oppressions of Nazism, were now fleeing the oppressions of Communism. Since my father had only convictions and no politics, of course he was furious.

So we moved to the west end, to the Kingsway, in fact—a district surely protected from these invaders by the regal authority of its name. We moved to White Oak Boulevard, a pleasant little street with tudor-type dwellings—in no way a boulevard—lined with red oaks! Three years later, when a Jewish family appeared on our street, my father moved again—on to Wimbleton Crescent in Islington. By that time, his commitment to the idiocies of suburban living was complete.

My father's return from the war corresponded with my early teenage years. By that time, I was beginning to creep away from the confines of my family and was separated from my sister in an acrimonious way.

As if to give me the prestigious education that, supposedly, all other Harcourts had received, when I was approaching the end of my public school days, my family had me sit for the University of Toronto Schools' entrance examinations. Although my sister was already at Bloor Collegiate, the deal was that if I were successful at UTS, she would be sent to St. Clement's—an Anglican girls' boarding school that also accepted day students.

I still remember the occasion. There was an endless series of examinations that were particularly humiliating. As far as I was concerned, they were asking me to play kindergarten games. I was to count to one hundred, utilizing only odd numbers, and was then asked to put pieces of wood into little holes. I was so angry and perplexed that I couldn't see the point of it. I didn't know anything about IQ tests! Nobody had offered me any preparation at all. In any case, I didn't get in. This failure meant nothing to me but severely disappointed my family. It rendered my sister furious. She felt I had betrayed her.

"Why should I be punished because you're so stupid?" she screamed. She was indignant. There was much biffing and shouting and very serious discussion as to what must be done. My failure, of course, was the cause of all this pain. Finally, in an uncharacteristic gesture of justice on my parents' part, my sister was sent to St. Clement's and I trudged off to Bloor. Though I continued to scrub her back in the tub virtually until the eve of her marriage, my sister and I were never fully close again.

I must say a word about Nellie. My Nellie, for that is what she was.

I have no idea who she was really. Nellie Hogger was a Cockney from Pimlico and was scarcely five feet tall. She had come out from the old country with bevies of other young women imported after the First World War as domestic help for Canadian homes. She had worked for some old girl in England who kept a gun under her pillow. Or so I was told. And did she also serve for a time at Buckingham Palace? It seems unlikely, but perhaps she had. In any case, if I felt a total love for my sister, Nellie felt a total love for me.

She bathed me and fed me and looked after me when I was ill. She didn't read me stories—there were no books in our house—but she recited poems that she had learned by heart. They were long narrative poems which I asked her to recite over and over again.

"The Fireman's Wedding" was my favorite. It was a tale of heroic deeds by a courageous fireman who saved a damsel from a burning building thereby earning her everlasting love. Was this the source of the fantasies I had in the hammock under the chestnut tree at the Hermitage in the summers? It seems likely. I used to have the same fantasy watching large chunks of anthracite burn in a wooden basket in the fireplace during the winters in our house on College Street in Toronto.

Nellie looked after me. I remember one night I had a hideous ear-ache. My adult molars were probably forming. Nellie stayed with me for hours and hours, reciting her poems and rubbing my back. She may have rubbed other things as well. I have a fragmented memory of my mother charging into the room one night and chasing her out. I don't know what was happening. But whatever Nellie did with me, I loved it.

Perhaps I should also tell about the end of Nellie. She worked all day and most of the night and when she went to bed in the evenings, she always wound up a Little Ben alarm clock that had long ago ceased to function. Its hands hung perpetually at half-past six. But the ticking was familiar. She needed it for company.

One Christmas, I who have no gift for giving gifts, deeply pleased her. When asked what she wanted, Nellie always replied that she would like a new pair of legs. I don't know how

I managed it but I found a little mannequin about a foot-and-a-half in length. I amputated the legs, wrapped them up with ceremony and presented them to her. She was extraordinarily moved. She always kept them on her dresser along side the alarm clock. Unlike my mother who always cried at Christmas, Nellie was rendered speechless by my gift of the legs.

After the war, when my family moved to the Kingsway, my mother wanted to let Nellie go. My father wouldn't let her. To be fair to my mother, the new house was not really big enough for a live-in maid and I believe my mother wanted to take over the cooking, as if to establish some worth for herself.

We were all teenagers by now and ate with our parents. Nellie ate in the kitchen, only a swinging door away. It must have been terrible.

I served Nellie dinner. One evening, while she was sitting in the little breakfast nook that was assigned to her in the evenings—she had become very small and frail—I was serving her meal and instead of pouring gravy, I drowned her mashed potatoes in the chocolate sauce that had been prepared for the ice cream. She ate her meal and didn't say a word. I think she feared it was a joke. Later, when I realized what I had done, I assured her it was an accident. She only partly believed me.

There was always a lot of tension between Nellie and my mother—even on College Street. But on White Oak Boulevard, they were constantly in conflict. I guess Nellie took badly at being deprived of her function, being left simply to dust and clean and do the washing up.

I don't know what happened. I think in frustration, Nellie tried to kick the cat. Instead she fell and broke her hip. I remember this tiny creature being carried away on a stretcher, crying out in panic: "This is the end of me."

She was taken to the Western Hospital on Bathurst Street. As my father was a doctor, he contrived to keep her there for as long as possible. It seemed like months. I visited her twice a

20

week and, of course, I was the only person she saw. Except my father. Neither my sister nor my mother visited her at all.

She was moved to a home at what was then called Five Corners, at the second intersection of Bloor and Dundas out by what is now Mississagua. I would visit her every Sunday, riding out on my bicycle to spend some time with her. I think she was happy in this home. It was the first time during her life in Canada that she had found some friends.

When I decided to go to England, Nellie was the hardest person to leave. I visted her one last time with my first great virginal love, Margôt. Margôt was about six feet tall. By that time, Nellie scarcely came up to her waist. I knew I had to leave and that I had to leave Nellie. But it was a wrench—for both of us.

I saw her once again—one summer when I was back. But during my first year at Cambridge, she died. My parents didn't tell me. They didn't want to worry me, they said. I think they were ashamed.

The home she had been in for a number of years changed hands. The new proprietors planned to institute a fee. Stingy in this as in all other things, my parents didn't want to pay. After all, Nellie wasn't family, as my mother explained. They decided to move her—to a home further away. She wouldn't go. She simply stopped eating and curled up and died. Later, when I participated in the death of my mother, I may have been taking revenge on her for this hideously insensitive act.

Two

So much of the past remains a blur. Flashes of things seen, echoes of things heard emerge from the darkness.

A sound that I shall always remember is the sound of horses

pulling delivery vans along College Street. Eaton's and Simpson's still used horses. The sounds of their hoofs on the rust-red road bricks must be one of my earliest memories; and while they took place in the city, they belonged to the country—like so much else in Canada in those days.

Horse-drawn vehicles persisted in the suburbs well into the 1950s, delivering milk and bread. No one who hasn't experienced these relics can imagine how they transformed city life, how they humanized it. They were such a living mediation between country and city, nature and culture, earth and world. Perhaps these anachronisms partly explain why so many Canadians, although living in cities, think of themselves in rural terms.

The other sounds that sit in my memory are the sounds of music. Yet how music began to speak to me is incomprehensible, just as, later on, I cannot imagine how books were, so insistently, to demand my attention.

My sister read books. I think she was even allowed to join the public library. For me, however, the library was out of bounds. "Books have germs on them," our family doctor once explained. "Stay away from them."

This wondrous philosophy of learning was put forward during a most peculiar autumn—an autumn during which my sister was deathly ill with scarlet fever. There was no penicillin in those days, and the whole house was quarantined from the rest of the world. All dishes had to be boiled and sheets and towels kept separate within the house. My sister felt so important but I was so bored.

Having received blood transfusions for an illness when I was two from my father and an Uncle Milt, I was immune. But I couldn't go anywhere because I might be a carrier. I certainly couldn't join the library or have anyone else bring books into the house. Far too risky. So I wandered about with nothing to do, imagining I was Tarzan or Buck Rogers. At least I was allowed to read the comics.

Music was another matter. My sister took piano lessons though they didn't "take" with her; but when she finally got to St. Clement's, she and a friend acquired enormous cultivation in my eyes by attending pop concerts on Friday evenings at Massey Hall. One time when her friend was ill, begrudgingly she took me along. Though I knew nothing then about "classical" music, I was thrilled not only by the sounds I heard but by the spectacle of the orchestra. All those instruments and people and that funny little man with his spastic gestures—it was Ettore Mazzolini—showing them what to do. To this day, the sounds of Tchaikovsky's *Capriccio Italienne* have a special significance for me. They take me back to my earliest discoveries of the spatial properties of sound.

I was no baby when these events took place. I was already at Bloor Collegiate and was beginning, in band class, to try to be a trumpet player. Although I was temperamentally unsuited for the most heroic of musical instruments, my struggles with its challenges were to dominate at least six years of my life.

My father, of course, wanted me to be a doctor. I didn't know what I wanted but I knew it wasn't that. I didn't want to be like my father.

Music became my great escape. It occupied innumerable hours, an infinity of days. It was a vehicle of perpetual avoidance. "I have to practise." This simple declaration saved me from so many things.

Music rescued me from most of the inevitable teenage humiliations. Through a chance encounter, someone got me listening to the CBC Saturday afternoon jazz broadcasts and he showed me how I could learn to play along. With its simple chromatic riff, *Tin Roof Blues* was the first tune I mastered. After that, there was no stopping my tentative improvisations.

This was the nineteen-forties. The jazz mantle had already passed from Louis Armstrong to Roy Eldridge and was being passed again on to Dizzy Gillespie and Miles Davis. Partly because I didn't have the technique to play flash nor the range to play high, I fluffed around a lot with my cup mute in. Someone told me I played like Miles Davis.

After that, of course, I began seriously to listen to Miles Davis. But I didn't play like Miles Davis. I played like me. Through my limitations, however, I played cool. Then I fell in with a collegiate music crowd. I joined the Don Young orchestra which played a lot of high-school dances. I played third trumpet (Don couldn't afford four trumpets) and played with trumpet greats like Ross Young and Kenny Sprang, both of whom became my friends. In fact, while I don't see him any more, Ken Sprang lives on in my memory as one of the most naturally gifted musicians I have ever known.

The Don Young band played all the major gigs, where cheer-leaders with their footballing dates would come up and talk to us. But we were cool—superior to the demands of sex. Later on, I formed my own little combo, the J.P. Harcourt Boppers. That was even cooler. In deference to our hero, Dizzy Gillespie, we all wore red berets that fitted like cow flaps, and tortoise-shell glasses, whether we needed them or not. Mine didn't even have glass in them. I simply wore the frames.

A guy called Vic Dickinson—not the real Vic Dickinson, although this one also played trombone—wrote his own arrangements and he too formed a combo. By this time, I was studying music at the University of Toronto and for Vic I played first trumpet (Vic could only afford one trumpet). I also doubled on piano, flute and bass.

God knows what we sounded like, but we got work. For two summers we played at Cleveland's House on Lake Rosseau in Muskoka and we all felt we were on our way. Where we were going, we had no idea; but we knew we were on our way.

The year I headed up Vic's combo, we went down to Bala one evening to visit our former drummer, Jack McQuade. He was then playing with Moe Koffman, and we all sat in. We jammed with Moe Koffman! That was the peak of my jazz-band years.

It seems impossible now, all that activity, all that music talk and music life and all that male bonding—guys together, getting drunk together, dreaming of getting laid. But I felt I was different. Perhaps I was just a snob. After all, I was a Harcourt and had been programmed for finer things. Not *educated*—simply programmed. There were other things in life that I had to discover. There was something else that I was driven to do.

I was so illiterate. So unread. In the jazz milieu, we all talked bop. The time we visited Jack McQuade, Moe made his first entrance coming downstairs from an afternoon nap. I remember his words. "There was a cat asleep on a pad upstairs, man, and that cat was me." We were so impressed. Real bop talk! So along with the red berets and the horn-rimmed glasses, we all aped the monosyllabic grunts of the great bop musicians.

Yet I knew there was something more, something other. Through a friend of my father, a CBC producer named George Young, I began to move in quite a different circle—not to move exactly but to nudge my way in gingerly. I didn't know what I was doing but I felt a kind of pull.

My father had asked Mr Young to talk to me. We talked about music, of course, although I have no idea what we actually discussed. But I do remember one thing. At a certain point, Mr Young said: "You're very analytical, aren't you?" During the rest of the conversation, I was paralyzed. I had to keep that word in my head so that I could run upstairs to consult my dictionary and find out what it meant.

Analytical. The word has stayed with me, both as a description and a curse. Being analytical, at the outset I was condemned more to criticism than to creation; and being analytical, I have introduced self-consciousness into everything I have done—even into my love relationships.

"I don't feel safe with you," my wife used to complain during the early years of our marriage. Perhaps she felt I would never have enough money properly to provide for us both.

Perhaps she was already beginning to recognize that, although she had been drawn to me, I wasn't the right man for her. But I think primarily she felt uneasy because I was so analytical, constantly analyzing everything that was going on between us.

Analytical I was and analytical I have been—for good and ill, for better or worse, in sickness and in health. However, through George Young, I met Geoffrey Waddington, then conductor of the CBC symphony orchestra; and through Geoffrey Waddington, I met John Weinzweig who—and I still can't believe this—agreed to take me on as a student in harmony. This was when I was still in high school.

So while bopping about with Ken Sprang and sitting in with Moe Koffman, once a week I assiduously prepared a chapter from Paul Hindemith's textbook on harmony, creating exquisite sounds for Weinzweig's approval even though I lacked the keyboard skills to play them adequately.

John Weinzweig was wonderful, less for what he taught me than for what he was—centred, dedicated, demanding and forgiving. Now in his eighties, he is wonderful today, for the music he has written, for the people he has inspired, and still for what he is—a stable force who is always in touch with his own centre of gravity, the man who imported modernism into the musical life of Canada.

Beyond all this music lay the world of words—the world of books and ideas. Because I was denied books as a child, it was late in life that I experienced the thrill of literature, of an imagined and imaginary world.

In Grade 10 while still at Bloor, I had been overwhelmed by the children's adventure book, *Cue for Treason*. Its evocation of Elizabethan England through a fictional contrivance was a first for me—an excitement even greater than that which I received at the movies. Although I have never since looked at it, I still remember the erotic thrill I experienced towards the end when the two boys were tumbling about together and one of them, by touching a part of the other that was different from himself, discovered that his friend was a girl.

Later on at Etobicoke, I was enormously influenced by my German teacher, a wonderfully courteous man called Harry Steele *mit einem großen Schnurrbart* who treated us all as equals; and in Grade 13 English, my imagination was seized by those two Miltonic chestnuts of institutionalized academe, *L'Allegro* and *Il Penseroso*. From Harry Steele has come my pedagogic belief that the most important learning occurs within an atmosphere of exchange among peers; and from those two poems possibly my addiction to dyadic couplings plus a strong conviction that people are driven as much by their basic temperaments as by any ideas that they might strive to adopt.

Even in my preliterate days, I must have had some gift of the gab—a fertile tongue—or I couldn't have impressed people the way I did. It is a mystery. The thought of being a changeling has always appealed to me. I cannot understand how I emerged from my home environment. My mother tells a story which marked me for life.

One day, during the war, she visited a psychic—someone who gazed in crystal balls, read tea leaves, and prophesied the future. She was supposed to be very good. I believe she had even been in trouble with the law for predicting changes on the stock market. In any case, the day of my mother's visit, uncanny things occurred.

The psychic began by rubbing her left shoulder as if in pain. "You're worried about your husband," she said. That wouldn't have been too hard to guess, given the fact of the war. But the shoulder was spooky. My father had suffered shrapnel wounds in his shoulder during the First World War, wounds that would give him trouble, especially when distressed.

There were other insights—or coincidences; but finally the psychic said: "You have two children." "Oh, no," countered my mother. "You're wrong there. I have three children." "Ah," returned the psychic, "you must understand something. Your son doesn't belong to you. He belongs to the world." She then went on to predict that I would become a great criminal lawyer or a brain surgeon or something like that, something that would take me away. That story has stayed with me because I have always been treated as if I were not really part of my family, as if I came from a different space.

Whatever all that means, however, it was through music that I was able, gradually, physically to distance myself; and it was also through music that I discovered the world of books.

I had experienced in school those scattered literary excitements; and one time when I was sick in bed, someone had given me some Dave Dawson books. But I wasn't a reader. Strange though it may seem, to this day I am still not a *real* reader.

I don't read easily. I don't read just for fun. Reading has always been work for me, even though work of a particularly joyous kind. Reading never involves distraction: it is always a quest for knowledge or an aesthetic elation.

Furthermore, concentration has always been difficult. I remember the autobiography of W.B. Yeats. Talking about his lack-lustre years at school, he explained: "Finding it impossible to attend to anything less interesting than my own thoughts, I was difficult to teach." For similar reasons, I have found it difficult to read.

Nevertheless, during my last years in high school, serious reading I began to do. I cut my intellectual teeth on the novels of Thomas Mann and Aldous Huxley.

I came to both through music. *Doctor Faustus,* I was told, was based on the music of Arnold Schönberg; and *Point Counter Point* promised a musical form. From these two books, I went on to read all of Mann and all of Huxley. With Mann I encountered the high seriousness possible in literature; with Huxley I discovered the powerful magic, the conceptual authority of words.

The words I read had nothing to do with the life I led. They had no acoustic presence for me. I had never heard them in speech.

Reading my way through Mann and Huxley, I would write words down in a little notebook, look them up in a dictionary, and try to memorize them. I would carry them about with me when I went for walks in the evening, striving to make them a part of me. I was learning a foreign language—the language of literacy.

I memorized whole chunks of Huxley, not through conscious effort but simply through reading them over and over again and sharing them with my friends.

Some sentences are with me still. "A beneficent providence has so dimmed my powers of sight that at a distance of a few hundred yards I am generally unaware of the full horror of the average human countenance." This was Huxley on *The Jazz Singer,* on the horrible ugliness of the movies, aggravated by the inescapably horrendous "Brobdignagian" blinks and smiles. For a full year or more, I lived inside Huxley's satiric, articulate world. Through Mark Rampion in *Point Counter Point,* I discovered the character of D.H. Lawrence; and from the fictionalized character, I discovered the man.

In fact, the life of Lawrence as presented by Huxley played a crucial role in the early days of my marriage. Like Mary and Mark Rampion, my wife and I wanted to walk across Europe in our bare feet, with knapsacks on our backs, shunning all possessions; and the first summer that we were married, this was our project. We wore shoes, of course, but walk we did. Hitch-hiking and walking. We were on our way to Sweden. First we would go north. Then we would go south. We wanted to map out the world.

I was exhilarated. I was in love. I was married. I felt, indeed (as I would later learn to recite), "primed for new scenes with designs smart and tall."

29

I don't know what my wife felt. Two summers previously with three of her girl-friends, she had toured Europe in a convertible. This year, she was walking. I think she more liked the *idea* of hitch-hiking than the painful reality of it. She too had been inspired by Huxley's portrait of the Lawrences, or perhaps more by my excitement at it; but she lacked my puritan necessities. She enjoyed the adventure, but deep down inside, she really wanted a bath and a sherry at the end of each day—something I couldn't provide.

We were both so young and idealistic. Our lives were deformed by literature. Learning that the Gladstones had read the Bible to one another on their honeymoon, we decided to read *War and Peace*. It took us a year to get through it, before moving on to *Anna Karenina* and then to Dostoievsky.

Except that the reading to one another didn't last long. Since I had never heard so many of the words, my wife spent most of her time correcting my pronunciation—yet another tribulation that we had to share. So she read to me and it was wonderful. I learned from her how to say so many intricate things.

My wife and I had met by accident. It was also by accident that I found myself one summer in the place where we would meet.

During my last year at university, I was hired to work at the Stratford Shakespeare Festival during its foundation year in 1953. I would be an extra but was also expected to work with Louis Applebaum to train the on-stage drummers for *All's Well That Ends Well*. That summer provided experiences that completely changed my life.

Here I was at Stratford—I who had scarcely seen a play! But I had seen some movies. I knew who Alec Guinness was and was soon to know people like Irene Worth and the formidable Tyrone Guthrie. Bill Hutt was there and Amelia Hall and Douglas Rain. And Timothy Findley. I couldn't believe my good fortune. Here were people who spoke like the books I was trying to read.

When I was swimming one day at a mini quarry half way towards the real quarry at St. Mary's, Guthrie arrived with some of his cronies. I was struck by the length of the man. He was over six feet tall. He had deep blue eyes that were matched by a tiny blue bathing suit that he wore about his loins.

I will never forget his first dive into the clear water. "It's gloriously tepid," he exclaimed on surfacing. I wanted to be around people who talked like that.

At Stratford, I had grown friendly with a young woman, Ann, who worked in the wardrobe department. Because I was involved with my girlfriend, Margôt, and although twenty-two years old, was still a virgin, Ann and I were just friends.

The last week of the festival, someone came to visit her. We were lolling about out back, behind the tent during a matinée performance of *All's Well That Ends Well*. I was dressed in my uniform of summer khaki shirt and shorts. Ann's friend appeared and I was bowled over. Her name was Joan—Joan Lucas from Montreal. She had a most exotic look about her. High cheek-bones, mischievous eyes, and a glorious tangle of blonde hair. She looked ready for anything. She was more beautiful than the screen women whom I most idealized— Mai Zetterling, Maria Schell. And the moment we met, we had our picture taken—outside the tent, beside a sign that cautioned "Performers Only". It felt like destiny. Indeed, in spite of all the troubles, it feels like destiny today.

There were also other elements in this cascading fate that was going to take me away from home, from Margôt and my Nellie, even, eventually, away from music.

At that time, music students at the University of Toronto had to endure many things. We had to pass a swimming test and we had to study English—for all three years.

Thank God for that imposition! During the first two years, trudging our way through a chronological survey, nothing I read in class meant that much to me. Nothing like Thomas Mann or Aldous Huxley. By our final year, however, we had reached the nineteenth century and were studying Victorian poetry with Claude Bissell and the moralists with F.E.L. Priestley.

The reluctant students would stroll into one of the large classrooms in University College, all the pass students who were obliged to take this course. Music and Phys. Ed. types thrown in together were reading *Varsity*, eating oranges, necking in the back row. No one seemed to care.

Taking us through the Victorian essayists, Priestley's contempt for this class was obvious. "Matthew Arnold was an educated man. Cardinal Newman was an educated man. *I* am an educated man," all his lectures implied. "But you swine!" The kids kept on reading, eating, necking. I, however, sat bolt upright in the third row, an insistent voice speaking within me: "Oink, oink, oink, oink!"

Even before Stratford and before I met Joan, I was beginning to realize that I would have to go to England were I ever to become worthy of all those mythical Harcourts who had gone to Ridley College, were I ever to become a proper embodiment of Arnoldian "sweetness and light".

During my last year at U of T, I sold my trumpet. That was the first of the precipitous castings-off I have performed throughout my life.

I walked into the old Conservatory cafeteria, in that wonderfully ramshackle building on the corner of College and University where the hideous Hydro erection now is, throwing ten-dollar bills into the air to anyone who could catch them. Although not yet at Stratford, I had already developed a flare for the theatrical, for the flamboyance of dramatized indifference. My friend Gaspar Chiarelli was running around behind me, gathering up as many bills as he could. "Peter's not quite himself today," he explained. Indeed, he was right. Peter was on his way to becoming somebody else. Or so he thought.

Inspired by Professor Priestley, excited by the books I was reading, I was still tormented because I didn't know what "literature" was. I knew it was important, but the classics meant nothing to me. Jane Austen, George Eliot, even Charles Dickens were virtually unreadable. There was a huge world out there that I didn't know.

And I was discouraged with my music. Not only would I never be a proper trumpet player—indeed, I no longer wanted to be—but all of music seemed just a little beyond my reach. I had started too late. I didn't have the ear. I lacked the manual skills to play any instrument adequately although I could play around with all of them.

Even though I had studied harmony with John Weinzweig, piano and composition with Sam Dolin, and had taken naturally to conducting, I felt inadequate. I would never be a "natural" musician like my jazz friend, Ken Sprang; and I would never acquire skills to be the equal of the people I so admired who were at the Conservatory at that time—Jon Vickers, Lois Marshall, even Glenn Gould who was hanging about studying composition, waiting until he was old enough to be professionally launched in New York.

When I discovered that I had been accepted by the English Department at University College to do a qualifying year towards an M.A. in English literature and had been appointed the conductor of the University of Toronto orchestra and chorus, I felt angry and unworthy. (I was also probably terrified.) How could I accept such an important appointment when I could scarcely improvise the chords for God Save the Queen? How dare they appoint someone so incompetent! Things were too easy in this little backward garrison, in this little corner of Canada.

Discontented with my abilities, I refused my success. I had to experience more. At Stratford, inspired by everyone but gently encouraged by Alec Guinness to become some sort of writer, I became convinced that it was a writer that I wanted to be.

And I had met the woman whom I wanted for my wife, who was on her way to England. I returned from Stratford, worked a mad two weeks at the Canadian National Exhibition and booked passage with Cunard Lines for late September. I bid farewell to Margôt, to Nellie, to my family, to music and off I sailed—saying goodbye to all that but determined, in the compulsive way that has characterized so many decisions in my life, to forge in the smithy of *my* soul the uncreated consciousness of *my* race!

I didn't know it yet, but I wanted to become a Canadian.

I haven't conveyed how unhappy I was. While I could be hysterically merry, often when alone I endured sustained attacks of melancholy. I believe I was an endogenous melancholic—*Il Penseroso* to the core. To this day, I still haven't sorted out this gloom—the tangled mixture of physical, psychological, and cultural elements.

Perhaps I was mildly hypoglycaemic. Depression always set in at the end of the day. Especially when I was working or was away from home, did I ever hate to see that evenin' sun go down. Had I known, I might have been picked up by a candy bar, as later on in life I would pick myself up with a tumbler of scotch.

Possibly my body had already been trashed by drugs. "Peace at any price," had been my mother's motto. Even when I was tiny, whenever there were any signs of external distress, my father prescribed tranquillizers. I was on phenobarbital by the time I was ten and have been on something similar ever since.

Unless chemically induced, sleep has always eluded me. During my self-dramatizing adolescent years, I used to think that I ought not to exist. After all, I was so covered with eczema from the day I was born that my hands and feet were tied to the four corners of my crib to keep me from scratching. Or so I was told. If this be true, it is no wonder that sleep and I have been uneasy partners.

I should have died at the age of two, I used to say to myself, when I was so sick with a strep throat that I had to have blood transfusions. I didn't want to think that my gloom was psychological. That would have implied a serious moral failing, a kind of accidie—a spiritual offence in the eyes of the Lord. I wanted to discover a physical cause.

When a trumpet player, I used to cite my inadequate embouchure as the source of my unhappiness—anything to avoid dealing with my inner sense of inadequacy. But by the time I had solved those problems, however, having spent a weekend in Philadelphia with Donald S. Reinhardt in order to adjust my embouchure and thus enable me to produce the fullness of sound that had always eluded me, I gave it up.

Inevitably in those early years, the gloom was also sexual, although it may have had more to do with the felt absence of love. Melancholy is always linked to a feeling of loneliness. If only I might fuse with another person, that would make me whole! This was certainly sexual but it was also part of a deep psychological need.

When I was tiny, it was as if I didn't exist. I lived through my sister. She made the decisions, imagined all our games. But she had grown up and moved away.

She had even got married. Worse than that, she had married a replica of my father. Simultaneously more cultivated and more authoritarian, he too was a doctor and was the kind of man who was accustomed to taking charge of things.

He sure took charge of my sister, finally moving her to an estate in the country where she had no-one to talk to and, once her kids were grown, had nothing to do. She became an alcoholic and recently died of cancer at the age of 62. Her domineering husband, although now in his seventies, was married again within six months. Even his kids were shocked beyond belief.

In a sense, all my life I have been looking for my sister, for someone who would imaginatively take charge of me. For a while Joan did that, with her exquisite sensibility and her love of reading—even of reading aloud to me. But she didn't want the job and there were other problems. These problems became the rust that ate away the centre.

The rust really grew from my sense of insecurity, from this pervasive feeling of inadequacy; and while I have sometimes been free from it, it is with me today.

People notice this. My wife noticed it. When trying to reach out for her, while trying to be intimate with her, I would feel her soul leave her body, as if to protect it from someone she couldn't trust. She may have sensed that part of me was missing. Perhaps that is why she never felt safe with me. Since I didn't know who I was, how could she know who I was? "I'd believe in you more," Joan used to say, "if you believed more in yourself." To which I wanted to reply, "If you believed in me, then I'd believe in myself." A hopeless, neurotic tangle!

Whatever the source of this emptiness, I have come to recognize that this feeling was also cultural. Having no sense of myself as a Canadian, I had no sense of myself as a person.

Throughout my five years of high school, there were only two references to Canada in all of my studies. One year, in English, we read a short story, *Essence of a Man*; at another time, in French, we read *Maria Chapdelaine*. I recall details of both texts because they spoke to me in ways that little else did. "No packer's grub, boss." A silly line of conclusion from what was probably a silly story; but it has stayed with me because it had something to do with the space in which I lived. "*Il s'est égaré*," was said of François Paradis; and I could imagine myself, trying to return to my beloved Maria Chapdelaine, getting lost in the woods.

At U of T, there was nothing. The survey course was strictly English literature; and except for Godfrey Ridout, all my music instructors were American. They were all graduates of the Eastman School of Music and the Eastman School provided all the texts we used. Perhaps even Ridout's comically boyish manner was the result of his feeling of Canadian inferiority, of his "younger brother" status within the Faculty of Music. Apart from my Jewish connections in the Conservatory—my work with Weinzweig and Dolin—there was nothing Canadian in what I did at all.

I don't know how this happens, but the culture one grows up in obviously contributes to a sense of self. It becomes a kind of mirror in which one sees oneself—or better still, a parabolic reflector that focuses a concentrated image of oneself. If the culture in question is ignored or denied, one is maimed in some way—imperfectly reflected, inadequately focused.

This situation is exaggerated if one hasn't grown up within an atmosphere of sustaining love at home. "Go away now, dear, and leave me alone," my mother used to say, "Your mother's tired. But remember, I love you." Such a pervasive double bind further erodes one's sense of self.

By the time I got to England, I had no idea who I was. I had left my friends, my music and my country in search of myself which, although I didn't yet know it, I hoped to find in the past. By going backward towards my roots, I hoped to find the soil in which I could blossom. In a way, I did. But it took a long time and caused a lot of pain, both to myself and to others. And in a sense, too, I became an artificial bloom.

Three

I set sail from the port of Montreal in mid-October in 1953. It was a tiny ship that would have been scuttled had it not been for the troop-shipment necessities of the war.

Except for Alec Guinness, I knew no-one in England. I didn't know where I was going or what I would do. I didn't know anything. With $200 in my pocket, I was off to conquer the world.

Ann, my friend from Stratford, and her friend Joan, came to see me off. They gave me the address of Andrée, another friend in London, so that was a start; and by a fluke, a young Englishman introduced himself to me before we had even left the port. His name was also André and, while working in Toronto that summer, had been staying with a friend of my mother's. André was terrific. We immediately became friends.

To André I owe everything. He was my constant companion during the ten days it took that little ship to cross the ocean. When we arrived at Southampton, André took me to London and put me up for a time. He also introduced me to some wonderful people, like his good friend Shosh, and the best restaurants in Soho—supremely Chianti's on Greek Street.

England was so familiar. I had seen it in the movies—in those Ealing comedies like *Passport to Pimlico* and *The Lavender Hill Mob*. There was a dinky-toy dimension to the place. Everything was tiny—the cars, the streets, even the trees. The whole world seemed more on a human scale—enveloping, self-protecting.

If Etobicoke was a wasteland, London was a womb. I felt contained there. Even the fog was comforting, like a familiar eiderdown. Coming to London was like coming home, coming to a home I had never had, a home before the Hermitage, to my grandparents' grandparents' house. I knew I belonged there. I felt secure.

And everything was cheap. In those days the rate of exchange so favoured the Canadian dollar that when I finally found a little room at the top of a house in Stafford Place overlooking—can you believe it?—Buckingham Palace, I was paying less than $10.00 a week. At that rate, I could live in London for ever.

I began to do things. More accurately, I began to discover the creative joys of doing nothing at all.

I had brought my bicycle and I cycled everywhere. I

mastered all of Inner London on my trusty CCM. I looked up Andrée and had dinner with Shosh and her friend, Helen Craig, a professional photographer who was the grand-daughter of Gordon Craig, the famous man of theatre. From all these young women, I learned the joy of cooking—and cooking in what was an exciting bohemian way. One of them, most kindly, even took me to bed.

I rang Alec Guinness. He was a bit surprised but very courteous. He too invited me to dinner.

I had been amazed to find his name in the phonebook and was even more amazed to discover how humble was his place. At that time he lived in a suburban dwelling by Shepherd's Bush with his wife and son. The night I visited, Richard Easton and Timothy Findley were there. Alec had brought them from Stratford to help establish their acting careers. We listened on the BBC to Kirsten Flagstad's farewell performance from the Royal Festival Hall. It was all very moving. I don't know who this Peter Harcourt was who was visiting that evening but I was sure he was on his way to freeing himself from the gnawing sense of the inadequacies of his past.

At that time, Shosh was studying theatre at the Central School, a wonderful place located in the Albert Hall. She put me on to the music program at the Guildhall School of Music and Drama. I wanted to acquire a performer's diploma and thought perhaps that I could gain one in conducting. I needed a diploma to complete my Mus. Bac. degree from the University of Toronto.

I have been suicidal, really, in so much of my behaviour. I had gained a straight "A" average in all of my courses and was the top student of my year in the Faculty of Music. But I needed at least a Grade 10 in my major instrument to receive my degree. Since I had been too arrogant to get it on trumpet, I now had to do it in conducting or improve my skills on the piano. Although I worked very hard and had splendid instruction in piano, finally, from a man called Sydney Harrison, I didn't quite achieve diploma standard and never have received my Bachelor of Music degree.

At the same time as I was working hard in music, I was trying to find out about literature. I wanted to grasp the culture of the past that I hoped might fill the hole at the centre of me. As my friend André was "reading" medicine at Magdalen College in Oxford, I visited him one day and met a gentle English don with the coincidental name of Robert Browning. He was sympathetic and very kind. He told me that if I wanted to study English, I should stay away from Oxford. I should go to Cambridge. That was where the action was. Robert may even have mentioned F.R. Leavis, but I knew nothing about these things. In any case, how could a young colonial from Etobicoke High School with no university degree ever get to Cambridge? This reach did appear to exceed my grasp.

Joan arrived in December; and that winter she, her friends Andrée and Sim and myself enrolled in a series of lectures at the Institute of Contemporary Arts. These lectures were terrific and really gave us all a sense of being a part of things, of being involved in an exciting, intellectual milieu.

All the media intelligentsia were there. There was Stephen Spender, the poet; Philip Toynbee, the journalist son of the famous historian; and A.J. Ayer, the logical positivist, who could speak with greater clarity and speed than anyone I have ever heard. There were also one or two others; but the final speaker was Dr F.R. Leavis, from Cambridge.

He looked like a man possessed, a bit like those traditional depictions of Paganini. With wiry eyebrows that jutted out from his forehead, he seemed so fierce and irreverent. Although I can't remember anything he said, I was enormously impressed. Here was a man who knew literature, who bestowed upon criticism a moral dimension, and who had no time for foolish courtesies. While he had worn a tie for his official address, he ripped it off even before he left the platform. This man, I said to myself, is the man I came to England to study with. I had to get to Cambridge.

Joan had another friend, Kathy, who was at Cambridge studying History. We went to see her. I arranged an interview at Downing College where Leavis was a fellow and was told that I could sit for the open scholarship examinations in the fall with all the Grammar School boys. So that is what I decided to do.

I had to write five exams—a general essay, a language examination (for which I did German), a history examination, and two English examinations. Along with working on my music, I began to study for these entrance exams. How did I have the nerve? How could I assume that I could possibly mug up all the necessary material, working on my own?

But I did it. I was amazed. To be fair, I think the college was somewhat taken with this naïve Canadian who thought that he could enrol at Cambridge as he had at the University of Toronto. But I was so keen, and the Commonwealth was still a family. Moreover, by the time I sat the exams, I was married and so wouldn't require a room in College.

Whatever the explanation, they let me in. Having acquired a wife, I was now going to acquire an education. Furthermore, for British subjects (as all Canadians were in those days), tuition was free. Still not knowing who he really was, I was off to Cambridge to study with F.R. Leavis.

No-one who has never met the man can appreciate his quality, his enormous moral force. Only traces of this force emerge from his writing, along with an apparent severity of tone. In spite of his many books, Leavis was not a writer. He was a teacher—and a teacher of an extraordinary kind.

Unlike most Oxbridge dons, Leavis held seminars with all of us at the same time. We literally sat at his feet, five days a week, sixteen weeks a year, for two years. We talked about literature. Or at least, Leavis talked. None of my English classmates ever said a word.

By the time I got to Cambridge in the mid nineteen-fifties, the Leavisian scene had become incestuous. Most of my fellow students had been trained in their grammar schools by Leavis graduates. They came to Downing well aware of the restricted canon and knowing by heart the party line. Perhaps there was no need for discussion. They were taking part in a ritual, like attending mass with the Pope. None of them ever took notes. That too might have seemed a sacrilege, like having to read from a book The Lord's Prayer!

None of this mattered to me. I was on a voyage of discovery through mysterious uncharted seas and as far as I was concerned, I had the best captain in the world.

I knew virtually nothing. I think I partly owed my acceptance at Cambridge to one particular text I had stumbled on in the public library when preparing for my exams. It was written by Wolfgang Clemen and addressed the development of Shakespeare's imagery, from his early to his late plays. It influenced me enormously and, for working with Leavis, it had influenced me in the right way.

The first day we all met together, Leavis expostulated on how, concerning the seventeenth century, there was so little to read. He mentioned H.J.C.Grierson's *Cross Currents in English Literature* and then said, "Of course, there's Mrs. Bennett's little book—*Four Metaphysical Poets.*" Everybody nodded slightly as if they knew it by heart. Meanwhile with great eagerness I scribbled down, *Formidable Civil Poets!* There were a lot of things I had to learn.

Although I had no such concepts at the time, Leavis was the exponent of an oral tradition, a tradition he celebrated as he equally lamented its passing away.

On several occasions he declared that "Education, Gentlemen, is at best a substitute." We should all have inherited the value system by which we make sense of the world at our mothers' knees or if not there, through verbal exchanges in the village, at the wheel-wright's shop.

Passéiste though such a longing might have been, it spoke

to me as a Canadian. After all, hadn't Canada been founded through a respect for tradition, through an honouring of the values of a different time? And didn't George Grant lament a similar kind of loss, as he too in his teaching embodied an oral tradition? Although at the time I didn't understand why, Leavis' celebration of what he called the organic community deeply appealed to me.

Leavis had been born on the banks of the Cam and had never really strayed from there. A Grammar School boy, he had been educated in Cambridge and went on finally to work at the university. But he was never made a university professor—the equivalent of a full professor in North American terms. He was even booted out of Downing College toward the end of his life—forced to retire I guess it was; but it was humiliating all the same.

The last time I saw him, he was sitting on the steps of the Fellows' Garden since he no longer had a room. Leavis made me realize that one could be radically traditional and still engender hatred. Everything Leavis did had enormous moral conviction. I guess that is what made him dangerous in the eyes of the establishment.

Like Socrates, he was feared as a corrupter of youth, as someone who, like George Grant in this country, felt the world was going in the wrong direction and that it was the role of education—in Leavis' case, supremely the study of literature—to maintain the values of fine seriousness that were slipping away. Hence his literary preferences—his valuation of Jane Austen over Henry Fielding, of George Eliot over Charles Dickens, of D.H. Lawrence over James Joyce.

Modernism was a problem for Leavis. It represented a purely conceptual literary enterprise, divorced from its roots in a national culture. Although his work is often related to what Americans were soon to call New Criticism, Leavis actually felt contempt for the purely aesthetic. So *Dubliners* was acceptable but not *Ulysses* let alone *Finnegan's Wake*. Similarly, it was largely the early work of Henry James, T.S. Eliot and

Ezra Pound that could be considered valuable, that played a cultural role. The rest was simply international showmanship, "all very well, of course," as Leavis would grudgingly concede, but of no moral value.

Dickens also posed a problem. Although in collaboration with his wife he was later to devote a full-scale study to the Dickensian achievement, at the time his only written comments were to be found in a short note on *Hard Times*. Even then, however, Leavis spent a lot of time with Dickens in class. It was the comic sense of the vernacular that excited him, and, of course, the human breadth of Dickens' world.

Reading aloud from *Dombey & Son* about Dombey's shock at having to introduce a wet-nurse into his house, Leavis would read out with delight: "Can't something be done with a teapot?". He would rock back and forth, his face red with laughter, holding his head in his hands. "Of course, Gentlemen," he would conclude, having celebrated a number of wonderful passages, "you can't take it seriously!" So except parenthetically, Dickens could not find his way into *The Great Tradition*.

Since he placed such faith in oral culture, Leavis championed those poets whose work was informed by a sense of the vernacular—John Donne and Shakespeare over Milton, Keats over Shelley, Browning over Tennyson and, supremely, a half a dozen poems by Thomas Hardy over practically any other poems in the immediate pre-modern world.

Leavis' own strengths were deliberately parochial. He celebrated those authors who were also parochial, who spoke to the culture from which they came. There were times when his parochialism bordered on intolerance.

Just as some people cannot bring themselves to say "fuck," Leavis couldn't mention King's College. For Leavis, King's College represented all that was effete in English letters and in university life. "Gentlemen," he would say, and there were often women in our class, "Gentlemen, even now, not a hundred yards from Great St Mary's, walking arm in arm with Dadie Rylands ... " And he would go on to express contempt for some King's College fellow, re-enforced, no doubt, by a suppressed homophobic rage. Similarly, Leavis so despised him that he would never mention by name E.M.W. Tillyard whom he always referred to as the Master of Jesus.

Leavis certainly had little respect for American academics. When discussing Matthew Arnold, Leavis had mentioned the study by the prestigious American critic, Lionel Trilling. "It's not too bad," said Leavis, "considering. Of course, he doesn't really understand him at all."

One day, Leavis cornered me after class. "My dear Harcourt, I hope you can help me. I don't understand American." Wanting to meet Leavis, Trilling had written him a note saying that he would be in Cambridge, Monday *through* Wednesday. "What does 'through' mean?" Leavis inquired. "I think it means inclusive," I replied. "I think it means that Professor Trilling will be in Cambridge from Monday until Wednesday," I added. Leavis looked disgruntled and depressed.

The next week, when we saw Trilling walking up and down with a college fellow outside Leavis' window waiting for the class to end, we were all excited. Would we witness the meeting of these two fine minds?

It was not to be. Leavis couldn't bear it. As the seminar continued, he became increasingly distracted. Finally, he broke off early and, pretending to be ill, climbed out the back window into the Fellows' Garden and then ran home along the Trumpington Road. He couldn't endure the academic interrogation that this American would engender.

Leavis' "great tradition" was an especially English tradition, although it also included "naturalized" foreigners like Joseph Conrad and Henry James. When still at Cambridge, I knew that Leavis' tradition was not the only tradition. Even

45

then I suspected that it would not be *my* great tradition. I still think, however, that it is *a* great tradition—one worthy of championing and setting apart from the rest.

They were magical, those years at Cambridge. By our second year, Joan and I had moved out toward Girton village—on Pepys Way, in fact—and people were always coming to visit. Friends would come up from London and we would go for long walks on Sunday mornings. Joe Melia, the actor, was a classmate of mine and he too would come out and keep us all in stitches. I think Joe was funnier as a friend than he has ever been allowed to be in his professional life.

As Cambridge is set in the fens, the surrounding country-side is flat. There was one walk, however, that involved some lovely hills, the brown earth chalked with streaks of white.

We would head off toward Maddingly, a good-sized walk, and then stop in a pub for a lunch of beer and sausages and searingly hot mustard. And, of course, we would play darts. It was wonderful. It was as if we had entered one of the novels we both loved so much. We were like characters from Thomas Hardy, striding across the centuries-old cultivation of the land.

As an ignorant Canadian, I think I enjoyed a special relationship with F.R. Leavis. He never took part in any student activities and deplored college productions of theatrical and musical events. Nevertheless, on one occasion, he made an exception.

Because of my work with a little choir that I had established at Downing College, offering British premières of *a cappella* works by Paul Hindemith and Heitor Villa-Lobos, I had been invited by some music students to conduct the larger college choir for the Christmas concert. Assembling the orchestra was itself a challenge and had its moments of hilarity.

When seeking out a trumpet player whose digs were at King's, I stopped at the Porter's Lodge to inquire about his whereabouts. "Hard by yon oak," the porter pontificated as he waved me on my way. At Cambridge, I often felt I had been thrown back in time.

As the evening of the concert approached, Leavis asked me about it. He was interested in having his daughter hear an accomplished flautist whom I had also acquired. "Well, I'm having my problems," I said, complaining about the resident organist. "It's going to take a miracle to bring it off."

The major work was a cantata by Bach: "Sing We the Birth,"—appropriate both for the Christmas season and for the fact that Joan was about to give birth to our first child.

I was very nervous. Not only had I never conducted anything so demanding but I also had to deal with this organist who was the college music scholar. I think he was miffed at my having been chosen and he further resented my flashy, North American ways.

He was to play the organ while I conducted the orchestra and choir. In Downing College Chapel, that meant that he was at one end and we at the other. As organists do, he played with his back toward the rest of us, taking his cue from my baton, when he consented to, by its reflection in a mirror. As a stubborn Yorkshireman with enormous keyboard dexterity, he felt under no obligation to look at me at all.

The evening came, the concert began, and everything went well. My organist was wonderful, catching my every cue. He had simply wished to terrorize me, to see if I would break so that he could take over. Certainly in college terms, the concert was a success. Not only was F.R. Leavis in attendance with his wife and daughter but he came up to me afterwards and grabbed me by the elbow. "My dear Harcourt," he said, "you've brought that miracle off." I was astounded and am still moved by the memory of that moment.

My favourite Leavisian anecdote derives from an encounter that occurred shortly afterwards. At the end of class one day, we were momentarily united by shared spousal suffering.

His wife, the formidable Q.D. Leavis, had been in hospital

receiving radiation for a suspected cancer and had been badly burned. Meanwhile Joan had almost died in childbirth, with bringing forth our daughter, Jennifer. Leavis and I were commiserating with one another about the state of our wives. Since I had been reading Conrad at the time, I made some comment about the remarkable tenacity of women. "Oh well," Leavis exclaimed, "women are like that. That's why you can't expect them to be intelligent too. When they're intelligent, they're really frightening. My wife frightens me."

I guess she did. One day, after a gaggle of us had been over to their house for tea, when seeing us out through the garden, Leavis asked me to slip down to the newsvendor's and pick him up a *Manchester Guardian*. "My wife won't let me have the *Guardian* in the house," he explained; "but perhaps I could read it out here for a while. I like to know what's going on."

People who have never worked with him can have no idea of Leavis' sense of merriment, his mischievous sense of humour. Even comments that might seem malicious can possess humour if one is able to imagine Leavis' searing eyes and tone of voice.

His attack on C.P Snow is a case in point. Snow had argued that the problem with the world today was the result of two cultures, one of the sciences and the other of the arts, with very little communion between them. Only exceptional people like himself, Snow implied, who as both a novelist and a scientist could properly understand the modern world.

This sanctimonious article threw Leavis into a rage. "C.P. Snow doesn't know the first thing about novels," Leavis wrote (and I am quoting from memory). "I don't believe he even writes them himself. I think they are written by an electronic brain called Charlie into which he programs the chapter headings." Nice malicious stuff, worthy of Dean Swift—an author whom Leavis once described as the most intelligent writer in English. But it was also playful and mischievous. It invited laughter and applause, on one level; but on another, it also demanded discussion of the future of the English novel and of the role that technology was now playing in the contemporary world.

Leavis got none of that. When the speech was published in *The Spectator,* the editors marshalled a whole army of *literati* to respond against it, fully in defence of Snow. That was one of the things we talked about, Leavis and I, when we sat out in the Fellow's Garden of Downing College the last time I saw him, after he had lost his room in college. "I don't think anyone will bother us here," he said, looking around nervously.

If great men are often paranoid, the treatment meted out to Frank Raymond Leavis both by Downing College and by Cambridge University toward the end of his days fully justifies any sense of paranoia he may have had.

From Leavis I learned far more than the value of literature. Selected literary texts were studied seriously in order to talk about the relation of the self to the social, the local to the universal and about the ultimate value of human life on earth. Fine writing was less important in itself than as an indication of moral health, both in the individual writer and in society as a whole. Before long, I was to champion similar values within film—initially addressing myself to the great European masters like Renoir, Buñuel and Bergman but eventually to the emergence of Canadian film.

What I gained from Leavis, finally, was something more abstract than specific literary skills. I learned to respect the excitement of intelligence, indeed the *danger* of intelligence, and to recognize the social isolation that can be inflicted upon anyone who approaches the world with exceptional knowledge and with intense moral seriousness. From F.R. Leavis, I acquired skills that would help me deal with the rest of my life in the rest of the world.

In *Six European Directors,* a film book I published in 1974, there is a footnote concerning the value of cultural ignorance when approaching works of art. This too may have its origins in an incident that occurred at Cambridge.

It was the end of my first year. Unlike Oxford, Cambridge held annual examinations, like the North American system. One of the papers entailed practical criticism. This was a technique developed by I.A. Richards but utilized by Leavis. It consisted of a sheet of unsigned bits of prose or poems that we had to compare and contrast, to evaluate as best we could, to date as closely as possible and to assign an author if we dared. It was a great exercise for drawing attention to the expressive details of style and to the shifting literary conventions of different historical eras.

For this particular examination, there was an Elizabethan sonnet and a fairly contemporary lyrical poem, both dealing with the ability of love to make life worth living. The sonnet was mechanically rhetorical and easy to dismiss as second-rate. But who could have written it? Sir Walter Raleigh? Fulke Greville? I didn't know; but I was convinced it was second-rate.

The lyrical poem, however, was magnificent. It is one of the most *perfect* poems in the English language. I can still quote it from memory.

Why do I go on doing these things?
Why not cease?
Is it that you are yet in this world of welterings
And unease,
And that, while so, mechanic repetitions please?

When shall I leave off doing these things?
When I hear
You have dropped your dusty cloak and taken your
    wondrous wings
To another sphere,
Where no pain is: Then shall I hush this dinning gear.

I was too ignorant to imagine who might have written it—W.H. Auden? I pathetically speculated—but I knew it was superb. The rhythmic authority of its run-on lines, its command of onomatopoeia and caesura, were virtually Shakespearean. Even the imagery, the "dusty cloak," was reminiscent of *Macbeth*. I was so excited. Not only did I feel I had written a good exam but I had discovered a great poem.

Afterwards, in the corridor, I heard my young colleagues talking in their superior, so-well-informed way. "Fancy putting a Shakespearean sonnet alongside a crummy poem by Thomas Hardy," one of them expostulated. "How dare they?" another complained. My excitement drained out of me. "Oh God, I've blown it!" I cried to myself. "I've failed!" The fullness of my self-confidence ebbed away and that corrosive Canadian emptiness returned. I didn't know what I would do if they threw me out.

In July that summer, in Montreal where Joan and I were visiting prior to the birth of Jenny, we secured the London *Times* to peruse the results of the examinations. Of all the students in my class at Downing College, I was the only one to have received first-class honours. While my duties as a musician and as a father didn't allow me to retain that distinction, I have retained the lesson I learned from that examination.

One must always be vigilant lest one's cultural assumptions get in the way of one's critical judgment—indeed, of one's intelligence. Later on, in the nineteen-seventies, when I found myself waging war against the increasingly dominant fashion of French film theory, I took solace from that important Cantabridgian event.

That summer, along with visiting our families, I was also seeking out sites either for employment or for graduate work. Since McGill was Joan's *alma mater*, I approached their English Department. We also went to Princeton, a place I was drawn to, partly through my admiration for F. Scott

Fitzgerald and his Princeton stories but also because of yet another incident concerning F.R. Leavis.

For a number of years, the English Department at Princeton had courted the great man, coaxing him to come out. "They offered me lots of free time and lots of money," Leavis explained, "the two things I hate." He wouldn't go. He didn't want to leave the banks of the Cam.

But I was really interested in McGill. The people there were courteous and encouraging. I was charting out a course that would return us to Canada.

But it was not to be—at least, not for a while. Although I did receive an offer of work from McGill, after we were all packed up and ready to go, at the last moment, it fell through. Since in my final year I had failed to retain my first-class honours, I knew that I would no longer be able to jump the queue toward an appointment at a Canadian university. I would have to go to graduate school like everybody else. Meanwhile, I had a family to support, plus another child on the way.

We returned, instead, to London. I entered the Ph.D. program at Birkbeck College as a part-time student and immediately found work as a teacher of English to foreign students. My friend André had himself married and had also started a family. He offered to share his house with us, the same house I had stayed in when I first came to England—22 Patterson Road, off the Finchley Road in N.W.3. Though Joan didn't much like the primitive nature of the place, I felt we would be okay.

Those were difficult years. Joan had given up her life for me. She had followed me to Cambridge and we had started a family, as one did in those days, so that she would have something to do. But the family was not enough. She wanted her own life. And we had not really bonded. We were never sexually close. Also, I began to realize that there were a lot of things about these conjugal mysteries that I still didn't know. I had to find out. I began to have affairs.

While this is not an aspect of my life about which I am

proud, initially it was necessary. Through checking things out with other women, I hoped to understand what was not working between Joan and myself.

This situation, however, was intensely diminishing for her self-respect as a woman. While I regret a great deal and wish that things had worked out more gracefully, I cannot imagine having done anything differently. Whatever the cost, I had to do what I did.

When studying the English Moralists, first with Professor Priestley and then with F.R. Leavis, I had been struck by much of what I read in J.S. Mill. I liked his sober understanding of the human condition, the way he had to struggle to find enjoyment in life. I was especially touched by his statement that it was better to be Socrates unsatisfied than a pig satisfied. When I was in my most miserable, melancholic moods, at least I could feel that, in some simple way, I was like Socrates unsatisfied.

Looking back on things now, I think that my sometimes joyful swiving bestowed upon me for a few moments that mindless condition of a pig satisfied. It gave me a sense of physical well-being such as I have never known in any other way. If only, I say now, I might have known that abandonment with my wife. If we might have known it together. But that too was not to be.

Four

After leaving Cambridge with my second-class degree, I was lost. I no longer felt a part of things. Cambridge had created such a finite world; and along with my studies, I had done quite a bit of music. I had even composed a score for a production of *Much Ado About Nothing* that Downing College put on.

Once again I assembled a consort of players, which I conducted during the performances. Louis Applebaum would have been proud of me. Needless to say, this time Leavis did not appear.

Once up in London, however, I felt exiled from that boundaried world. While I did propose some theme music for a dramatic series at ABC Television out in Teddington, it was not accepted. My music began to lapse. In any case, there was my teaching and my children. While I wasn't sure exactly what I would be doing with the rest of my life, there was too much going on for me to be as fretful as I had been in the past.

However, I still found time to experience gloom—especially within my marriage. As an escape, I retreated into cinema.

Although I had seen a lot of movies growing up in Toronto and had even experienced some "art films" there, I scarcely ever went to the cinema at Cambridge. Neither Joan nor I had the time or the money—or, for that matter, the interest. We weren't at Cambridge to see movies.

In London, however, I discovered the National Film Theatre. It was tucked away in a small space on the South Bank under Waterloo Bridge. I was immediately struck by the warmth of its design and by the ordered nature of its programming. The first season I attended consisted of Austrian films—of films about Vienna.

I saw some silent films by Erich von Stroheim and some stuff by Max Ophüls—a director whose work, except for *La Ronde*, I scarcely knew. I was entranced. These weren't the mindless movies I had grown up with in Canada. This was cinema. This was art.

The next season was called "The Passionate Cinema." It consisted of about 40 Swedish films from the nineteen-forties and nineteen-fifties, Sweden's "second golden period" as the program notes explained. Evidently there had been a vibrant silent period headed up by two great masters—Victor

Sjöström and Mauritz Stiller. Sjöström would become familiar in North America as Dr Isak Borg in Bergman's *Wild Strawberries*, and Stiller is still presented in the American film histories as the man who brought with him to Hollywood a beautiful Swedish shop-girl named Greta Gustafsson who would later be known as Greta Garbo.

This Swedish retrospective took place in 1957. Ingmar Bergman's *Smiles of a Summer Night* had been a success at Cannes a couple of years previously and *The Seventh Seal* had just been a hit in New York. Bergmania was about to begin. However, the NFT season was not just about Bergman. Although he had already made over a dozen films, all of which were being shown for the first time in London, there were also films by Alf Sjöberg, Arne Mattsson, Gustav Molander, Anders Henrikson, Hasse Ekman—all kinds of people. What struck me about these films is that they were all exactly the same! At that time there was an enormously homogenous culture in Sweden that spoke its values from the screen.

I had already been attracted by Strindberg and Ibsen and had been excited by the scarlet paintings of Edvard Munch. Moreover, because of my childhood experiences at the Hermitage, I found in these Scandinavian works more sources of personal identification than I could from the novels of Ernest Hemingway or D.H. Lawrence. With their tormented puritanism, these Scandinavian works spoke to me in very private ways.

So did all those Swedish films. I was extremely excited. My graduate studies at Birkbeck College were not engaging me. After F.R. Leavis, Professor Tillotson was a wanker—everything in English letters that Leavis had taught me to despise.

During our first seminar at Birkbeck, for instance, a seminar that was devoted to a textual study of *The Ring and the Book*, the long narrative poem by Robert Browning, Tillotson met us with a morocco-bound copy of the text. The first thing he did was to drop it ceremoniously three times on the table. Thud, thud, thud! "The weight of it alone," he said with profundity, "is astonishing." I was sure by then that English literature was about other things. I never went back.

In any case, I felt that the most fertile fields in English literature had already been ploughed. These Swedish films supplied a new challenge. I sought out the British Film Institute, the organization that ran the NFT, to find out more about these wonderfully neurotic films.

The BFI was then a tiny clutch of offices on Shaftsbury Avenue, just up from Cambridge Circus. It housed an extensive book and periodicals library and a collection of stills. At first I was shocked to find a rather loud-mouthed American very much in evidence. What was *he* doing there? I wanted British things to be British as, in a way, I still do.

This loud-mouthed American I was soon to know as Richard Roud, a man of enormous knowledge and passion for the cinema and one of the most courteous of all the people whom I was soon to meet and who would shortly become my colleagues. Richard was the programmer of the NFT. He was the person responsible for all those Swedish films.

Going through the material on Swedish cinema at the BFI, I quickly discovered there was nothing to read—certainly nothing substantial in English. Six months later, I was famous! Or at least, I was well-known.

That is how things happened in England. If you managed to get access to a particular newspaper or to the BBC, everybody knew you. The sceptred isle is so tiny and the media were so controlled. It was wonderful, even if it had to change. With only two television and three radio outlets, everybody in the country listened to you once you got on the air.

I prepared an article contrasting Bergman's *Summer Interlude* with some American film, proving to my great satisfaction the cultural, artistic and moral superiority of the Bergman. I sent it round to everybody and began the writer's apprenticeship of dealing with rejection slips.

One day, however, I got a letter from a producer at the BBC, praising my insights but adding that they weren't particularly broadcastable. "Yours etc.," in the British way. I wrote back saying that if those comments in praise of the piece weren't simply English hypocrisy (I have always been noted for my tact), let us make it broadcastable. We set up an appointment and we talked about the possibility of my preparing something for the BBC on the films of Ingmar Bergman.

I can tell Richard Keene stories the way I tell F.R. Leavis stories. He was so knowledgeable and caring; and since there was to be a season of Bergman films at the Everyman cinema in Hampstead, Richard decided to put me on the air.

First he worked on my prose. Whatever Leavis had given me, he had not stressed elegance of style. Richard would read through my stuff out loud. "What an interesting sentence," he said at one point. "What a wonderful interplay of adjectives. You balance them all so extraordinarily well." I sat there, glowing inwardly, taking pride in such a kind reception to what I had written. "However," he went on, "*which* adjective would you like the listener to retain?"

Thus we went through it, simplifying it, focusing it, making it read like speech. There was also my voice to work on, with its sibilant "s" and foreign way of saying things. For that first broadcast, Richard Keene spent four hours getting fourteen minutes of my excited critical nonsense on to tape. I was enormously impressed and, of course, enormously grateful. That single broadcast set me on my way. I was a professional—an authority on Ingmar Bergman!

My work on Bergman flowed directly from the work I had done at Cambridge—indeed, directly from the work I had done on Shakespeare's imagery in order to get into Cambridge. Both by temperament and training, I recognized that the achievement of Bergman lay less in his creation of characters than in his construction of a poetic world in which every element was expressively as important as every other element. *Summer Interlude* was, I argued, Shakespearean in design. It had to do with youth and age and with the recurrence of seasons. "By having crows answer cuckoos," I suggested, "and medlars follow strawberries, Bergman not only moves us by the strong emotional effect of these sounds and images but he thereby distances the action sufficiently from real life to enable us to be conscious of it as a work of art."

A week later, Joan and I were in the queue for yet another Bergman film at the Everyman when we heard a couple talking in front of us. The guy was explaining to his companion how he had heard this bright American on the BBC the other evening who really understood Bergman. We were both thrilled. I didn't even mind being mistaken for an American.

After that initial broadcast, I did occasional radio reviewing. I also placed some pieces in a nineteenth-century magazine called *The Twentieth Century* and later in *The London Magazine.* I had the knack of reading through a few issues of such periodicals, grasping the stance and tone, and then submitting book or film reviews, which were then accepted. Before long, I was doing the same for *Sight & Sound.* In those days, I possessed the skills of a journalistic ventriloquist.

However, whenever I did anything that came from my heart, from my bowels, in fact, it was either re-written or rejected. During the eight years that I was associated with *Sight & Sound,* six of them while working for the BFI, Penelope Houston accepted only one article that had been personally devised by me. All the rest was commissioned work.

But that article was prophetic. It was about the National Film Board—my first piece about Canada, written in 1963.

When I decided to give up my university aspirations and seek a proper teaching position, I worked first at Kingsway Day College and then, through the Kilburn Polytechnical Institute, at the London Police College in Hendon. My sponsor in these jobs was Fred Flower—a person who is still an inspiration for me.

I had first met him when he was in charge of English Studies at Hendon Polytechnic and I was still teaching English to foreign students. When Fred became principal of Kingsway, he took me with him.

All these institutions were engaged in what the British euphemistically called "further education." Actually, it was stop-gap education, remedial education. It was designed to deal with "day-release" students—with kids who had quit school for work but who had to return to an educational program for one day a week, at their employer's expense, until they were sixteen.

As Fred wanted to devise dynamic offerings for these kids, he attracted to Kingsway a number of young people, none of us professional teachers, many of whom had North American accents. The assumption was that since we hadn't been formally trained, we would have new ideas.

My job was teaching literacy—to kids who didn't want to know. They had dropped out of school because they hated the system. "Literacy" belonged to the upper classes. Literacy had been taught to them by guys named Austin and Jeremy but they all had names like Alf or Joe or Bill. Literacy was the power wielded against them. Literacy was the voice that told them what to do.

The old techniques were hopeless. The available books useless. You know the kind of thing: we have all been through it. A story or a poem and a list of exhortations: "Describe the theme and central thought." Deadly! Even if they were literate. That was when I began to bring in films.

Film was their medium. Everybody went to the movies. If you showed a film in class, everyone talked about it. They all had something to say.

There were a lot of other games that we played—media games, as we might call them today. I would have different groups take notes of a set discussion, as if they were reporters for the telly. They would write up their findings and, of course, each group would discover that they had reported different things. I had them write reports on different aspects of the school or, sometimes, of their jobs—whenever possible, working together in teams. Anything to keep them writing, to get them using language to analyze their worlds. Finally, I had a brainwave: we would make a film.

I didn't know a thing about filmmaking at the time but ignorance has never stopped me. Fred found some money and we set to work. Individual students had to write about different aspects of the school—the gym, the cafeteria, the classes, the play-yard. Someone had the brilliant idea of using a girl's legs as a continuity device, her white boots moving from place to place throughout the school, as if looking for somebody.

I don't know how we did it, but we got a camera, shot the film and generated enormous excitement throughout the entire school. Even the old-guard was impressed. Pedagogically, however, what followed this production was even more important.

At the time, a virtual renaissance in film was under way. Largely as a result of faster film stocks and lighter equipment developed for television, a new kind of documentary was beginning to appear. With the launching of Ilford HPS, it was possible to shoot on the streets at night without lights. There was a sense then, as there is today with Hi8 video, that anyone could make a film.

In England, Lindsay Anderson, Karel Reisz and Tony Richardson were making their first short films, as were Claude Chabrol, François Truffaut and Jean-Luc Godard in France. Initially, these shorts were all programmed together at the NFT under the collective banner of "Free Cinema." People now felt free to make personal statements on film.

A number of these films were concerned with young people or with people in the streets. *Nice Time, We Are the Lambeth Boys,* and *Momma Don't Allow* were typical. At Kingsway Day College, when I brought these films into class, the students saw them in an entirely different way. From the insights gained in the process of film production, the kids could see the holes in the productions of other people. The process of filmmaking had been demystified. None of these young people ever saw films in the same way again.

The value of this exercise at Kingsway Day College was to be confirmed a few years later when working with the inspirational Douglas Lowndes at Hornsey College of Art. It would further inflect the priorities of the film studies program at Queen's University, which I established in 1967.

Many of the students at Kingsway Day College were in training for the police force. When the police decided to set up their own college specifically to educate kids for the force, on Fred's advice I applied for the job. To my great surprise I was hired. Since it involved designing a new curriculum especially for young coppers, it was an enormous challenge. I was doubly excited because, finally, I had a full-time job. I could buy a house, settle down and look after my family. No sooner had we moved in, however, than Joan took the kids and herself back to Canada. It was called a visit, but I knew the visit would last a long time.

I only worked at the police college for one and a half years. That was enough. It was as close as I ever came to being in the army.

I certainly don't regret it. Sociologically, it was an experience. Educationally, however, it became more and more conventional. By the end of the first year, the officers had abandoned their policy of designer education and wanted to train the boys to do "O" and "A" levels like everybody else. I was beginning to feel unfulfilled.

I was, however, doing more and more work in film. Through the intercession of Thorold Dickinson, the retired British film director who, with Sir William Coldstream, had set up the first film study program at university level in Great Britain at the Slade School of Fine Art within University College in London, I was introduced to Molly Lloyd at the British Film Institute. She ran the freelance lecture service, finding people to speak on different aspects of the cinema for film societies, Workers' Educational Association meetings and weekend study groups.

I became a travelling minstrel. I trekked up and down the country, talking about film music, about Ingmar Bergman, about the new British cinema and the French New Wave— even on one extraordinary weekend, about Westerns about which I knew nothing at all!

But neither did anybody else. We were approaching the film age, the age of the nineteen-sixties. Everybody was hungry for more knowledge concerning what was going on.

Paris was the centre of this growing excitement. It was Paris that discovered the American cinema, that programmed it systematically and produced articles and books about its achievement. In England, if you read *Cahiers du Cinéma* and then *Positif* for a contrasting point-of-view, you were an authority on all matters cinematic. Having read as well a handful of French books, I became an authority apparently on everything.

And of course, I was "analytical." Although with age I have found it increasingly difficult, I was a natural teacher. My work as a musician made me a willing performer; by now I had received a good education; and films did seem to be my medium. They combined all my various interests and reached to the depths of my soul.

Not only was music a part of film, but the narrative structures of European films were often musical in organization, with their different modes, pitches and rhythms. Films also created the sense of a social world, apparently direct representations of a living reality. They seemed so much more immediately than language to convey the particularities of an actual culture.

As in literature, there was imagery; as in painting, visual design; as in drama, characterization; and as in music, pulse, energy, rhythm and movement. Film brought together my interests and abilities and focused my attention more than any other medium. Furthermore, since the cinematic fields were still so uncharted, there seemed such a lot of exploratory work that needed to be done.

My Cambridge education provided a superb preparation for this task. Not only had Leavis encouraged us to relate art works to the social world, but Part Two of the English Tripos encouraged us to relate the critical disciplines of literature to other aspects of culture or, indeed, to other cultures—even if in translation. That was when I was systematically exposed both to ancient Greek drama and to the plays of Strindberg and Ibsen. I felt well prepared to take on the burgeoning art of cinema.

It is not surprising, therefore, that when a job came up within the Education Department of the British Film Institute, I was the guy they hired. A friend had introduced me to Paddy Whannel who was the Education Officer. He had also been quite active in the first phase of the *New Left Review,* a magazine of progressive political thought that had been born from the ashes of the Suez fiasco in the nineteen-fifties. Stuart Hall was the editor, and people like E.P. Thompson and the Canadian philosopher Charles Taylor had been involved.

Paddy was impressed both with my credentials and with the fact that I had been a jazz-band trumpet player. He felt that was a humanizing factor, somewhat mitigating my "elitist" interests in cinema.

Paddy was interested in movies. Most of all, he loved musicals. And he was devoted to education. His goal was to get film courses established in the secondary schools. His strategy was to target teachers, to work at the level of the teacher-training college to create an interest that would then trickle down to the schools.

We got on wonderfully together. He was a drinking man, a swiving man; and while his interests were with the working class, as a Scot he was classless. He was also refreshingly frank about everything he did.

For the six years I worked at the British Film Institute, I felt more centred than I ever had in my life. After a prolonged visit to Canada, Joan returned, although I don't quite know why. I think she found it hard to make a go of it on her own. And the kids missed me. At least, Jen missed me—my son scarcely knew me. We all wanted to try to rectify that lack.

I was also more positive. I was at the centre of things. I had a job. I had a house. I had been to a youth festival at Cannes and to a Summer School at St. Andrew's. While I could still be very gloomy, especially when left on my own, I felt that I was beginning to take charge of things. I was writing more and more—shitty little things, really, largely for *Sight & Sound*—but that didn't matter. I was active. I even had a car. I must have sounded positive in the letters I sent home.

For the Extra-Mural Department of the University of London, the British Film Institute organized evening courses in film. I taught one of them. This course formed the nucleus of what was later to become *Six European Directors.*

I had, at this time become excited by Herbert Read, the English educational thinker and critic of art. Read's *Education Though Art* influenced me enormously, as it had the teaching of art in Great Britain. A Jungian analysis of children's drawings, it encouraged me to think of film artists in similar ways. So Bergman was not only Swedish while Renoir was French; Bergman was also an "introvert" while Renoir was an "extrovert." I didn't apply the grid mechanically, but through Read I was encouraged to think of the work of individual artists as stemming not only from a particular culture but also from a bias in the artist's personality. It was *Il Penseroso* and *L'Allegro* again.

While not refusing value judgments as, later, the structuralists were to do, this approach did encourage a tolerance for the self-indulgences of Bergman and Fellini. Furthermore, since neither of these artists was much acclaimed in the politely repressed high-brow culture of Great Britain, I was encouraged to tilt against the received assumptions of the establishment press. While I didn't know it at the time, these strategies were to stand me in good stead when, later on in life, I was to discover Canadian film.

One summer, after I had left the BFI and had been hired by Douglas Lowndes to work with young filmmakers at Hornsey College of Art, I arranged a holiday for my family. Since I had already begun to explore still photography and had even taken an evening course in film production at what was then the Regent Street Polytechnic, Douglas gave me an 8mm Bolex and a Uher tape-recorder and commanded me to make a film. This film would qualify me as a production instructor!

Douglas was like that. He believed in keeping things simple. Unlike many production personnel I would later meet, especially in the nineteen-seventies while teaching at York University in Toronto, Douglas creatively down-played the mysteries of technology. Keep it in focus, expose it correctly, think about what you want to do and go and make your film.

While in Devon with my family, I produced a dawn-to-dusk study of the fishing village of Appledore. This exercise gave me my first thrill of making cinema, of controlling light and sound and movement and colour. The film wasn't much but the experience was wonderful.

It was about this time that I began to think of returning to Canada. While everything was going well, or so I believed, other factors had conspired to make me feel that I could never get my life together with Joan and the kids until I found a job back home.

Although there was no longer the same need, I had become involved with another woman—a young woman she was and the relationship between us had become much more than an affair. Even Joan thought she was lovely and the kids adored her. While she never actually lived with us, the relationship was so close that it was virtually a *ménage à trois*.

Margaret is physically the most loving woman I have ever known. If with her exquisite sensibility Joan was like my sister—someone I adored but couldn't really possess—Margaret was my Nellie Hogger. I have never felt so loved by anyone in my life.

She had the courage of commitment. She used to say that you had to be prepared to leap over a cliff. One time on a holiday together, when in my foolishness I nudged us both to leap over an actual cliff, she almost drowned. But she was like that—full of trust and love.

Close as we were, however, there were other forces keeping us apart. Most of them were internal. They were endemic to the way I constructed us as a couple—not as a substitute for but as an addition to my marriage. I felt that I could resolve this situation, so wonderful for me but so unsatisfactory for both Joan and Margaret, only by returning home.

There were also other factors that made me want to come back to Canada. While still at the BFI, one of my jobs had been to supervise the certification of educational films. If foreign films were deemed educational, they were imported without tax.

Through this activity, I began to see films made by the National Film Board—nostalgic films like *Corral* and *City of Gold*; philosophical films like *Universe* and *The Living Machine*; incisive, "direct cinema" films like *I was a Ninety-Pound Weakling*, *The Days Before Christmas*, *The Back-Breaking Leaf* and the fabulous *Lonely Boy*—a film about the early success of Paul Anka.

These films really excited me. Having been in England for over ten years, I had become accustomed to thinking of myself as a North American—a citizen of the world. These films challenged this esperanto position. Looking at them I said to myself: "These aren't American films. They're not British films. They must be *Canadian* films." From the aspect of self-recognition that these films provided, I wanted to return home.

What the films possessed was a sense of detachment, a reflective tone. They inquired into the meaning of life while exposing its absurdities. They were the product of a sensibility that looked out at the world without being a part of it. In this way, they were Canadian. Bit by bit, they began to change my life.

They were actually all the product of one unit at the Board—the much applauded Unit "B." In the summer of 1962, I made a trip back to Canada to research this team but also to explore the possibilities of a permanent return.

My visit to the Film Board was chaotic but wonderful. I had also visited the Canadian Film Institute in Ottawa. Roy Little and Peter Morris had been most welcoming and had set up an appointment at the NFB.

I was treated like a foreign dignitary—Peter Harcourt of *Sight & Sound*! Some pleasant, perfunctory person in the PR department offered me the royal tour. "Of course, you'll want to meet Norman McLaren," he said to me. "No," I replied, no doubt with my characteristic hostility, "I don't want to meet Norman McLaren. I want to meet the guys who made *Lonely Boy*." "Who are you," I believe he complained, "*not* to want to meet Norman McLaren?" We were not getting on.

Indeed, except for the films of Norman McLaren, the Film Board has never known how to deal with its most distinguished product. My PR guide abandoned me and I was passed over to a generous woman called Lucille Bishop who understood what I wanted. "Everybody's in studio today," she explained. "But if we sit in the cafeteria, they'll all have to come in, sooner or later." So that is what we did; and one by one, they all came in.

Bob Verrall was there and Wolf Koenig and Roman Kroitor; and then Colin Low and, of course, Tom Daly who, as

Executive Producer was the king pin of Unit "B."

I asked questions and they told me things. I in turn told them about how much I admired their work—even *The Living Machine* Part 2, a film that officials at the Board found particularly embarrassing. "You must be a highly intelligent and sensitive young man," Roman said to me, partly in jest. He was the man most responsible for that film.

Within this unit, however, they all worked collectively, deciding on the credits when the film was finished. After Terance Macartney-Filgate left the Board, Wolf did most of the shooting and Marcel Carrière grabbed the sound. But they all worked together, no doubt under the benevolent dictatorship of Tom.

It was marvellous. I was not only discovering the films but I was rediscovering myself. I was apprehending my country through the work they had done.

They thought I was nuts. They didn't perceive themselves as doing anything exceptional. They didn't even perceive me as Canadian. Furthermore, at the time there wasn't much serious comment on film—certainly not on Canadian film.

When my article appeared in *Sight & Sound*, while my Unit "B" friends were pleased, the Film Board was embarrassed. I had implied that some of their films were better than others. I stirred up resentments within other units at the Board, the ones that made the dull films on beavers and wheat. I don't know to what extent I was the cause, but shortly afterwards, the unit system was abandoned.

A few years before these Film Board experiences, just after I had come down from Cambridge, my wife and I attended a jazz concert with some friends. It was the great Duke Ellington concert on the Edgware Road—his last British concert before he died.

Our friends were all graduates of Queen's University and with them, staying in England for a year while working on his Ph.D., was one of their favourite profs—the now highly esteemed Canadian political scientist, John Meisel. We immediately got on. Joan and I found both John and his wife, Murie, immensely sympathetic. Meisel was drolly humorous and at the time somewhat resembled Groucho Marx, a resemblance he liked to cultivate.

His thesis examined the landslide electoral success of John Diefenbaker's Conservative Party in 1956. Meisel was worried about his principle player. "After researching this guy's life for over two years," he once exclaimed, "I've discovered that his contact with reality is discontinuous!" A university professor who talked like that I could certainly relate to.

Meisel was probably extremely taken with Joan, as everyone tended to be, as I certainly was. But whatever the explanation, we became friends. We sometimes went to the ballet and had meals together. When they returned to Canada, we kept in touch.

After the excitement of my Unit "B" experience, I tried to imagine what might get me back to Canada. I immediately thought of Meisel. I sent off a letter accompanying our annual Christmas card inquiring when Queen's University was going to set up a film program. Within weeks I received an invitation from George Whalley of the English Department inviting me to return. So in the summer of 1967, having lived fourteen years in England, my wife, my daughter, my son and myself all returned to Canada.

Five

After considerable deliberation, Joan and I decided that she should go on ahead with the kids. We didn't want them to see their London home dismantled. I took them to the airport to set them on their way.

69

No sooner had they passed through security than I experienced an extraordinary elation. In part it came from the adrenalin of control, of feeling master of my fate. But there was something else as well—something to do with the future, with the excitement of new possibilities in life.

But that wasn't all. When I came downstairs on my way to the car park, I noticed someone at a newsstand. He was tall and thin and very old. He had a beard, a slightly crooked smile and a bump on one side of his forehead. I knew this man and I knew him from film.

He caught my stare and approached me, his right hand extended. "Warren McCulloch," I managed to exclaim as we reached out and shook hands. "I've seen you in the movies. All those National Film Board people are friends of mine," I said, over-simplifying the matter. "For heaven's sake," he replied and then passed into the Pan Am section on his way to the United States.

Dr Warren McCulloch was a cyberneticist at the Massachusetts Institute of Technology and, indeed, I did know him from the movies. I knew him from *The Living Machine*, one of the very films that had been instrumental in encouraging me to return home.

Return home. Once again, I was acting compulsively. I was leaping over a cliff and I was taking my family with me. Burn all bridges and get away! That was my plan. For Joan, I was later to learn, it felt like a death sentence. For me it was ecstasy.

If my years in Kingston were the most productive in my life, they were also the most destructive. It was a wonderful time for film and a terrible time for marriages.

In the nineteen-sixties, film was everybody's favourite subject. Along with the happy music of the Beatles, film was what we all had in common. In Kingston, however, as if trying to catch up with the free-loving hippies, very soon what we also had in common was one another's wives.

Looking back now from my male perspective, I think that

everybody lost. We all lost something. We lost our innocence. We lost a part of ourselves, a part of the integrity of our imagined worlds. "Divorce is like an amputation," Margaret Atwood once wrote. "You survive but there's less of you left." If my early affairs had been unavoidable, none of this Kingston chaos was necessary at all.

Moreover, my first year in Kingston was the happiest I had ever known. I was only an occasional drinker and I slept without drugs. Yet I was seduced into shattering this serenity. Having all, I wanted more. Once again—suicidally—I was leaping over a cliff. I was throwing everything away.

The women didn't see it that way. They didn't want more: they wanted change. Betty Friedan's *The Feminist Mystique* was, along with John Updike's *Couples*, everybody's favourite reading—the yin and yang of Kingston's literary interests at the time. Women were beginning to realize that they no longer had "to go on doing these things." They wanted out. They wanted their freedom; but as one grows older, freedom often becomes the freedom of living alone.

In the nineteen-sixties, however, it was as if everything was beginning. The turning away from Vietnam toward the flower generation seemed to herald a more loving society; and the celebration of popular music and the movies across the generations did seem to promise an extraordinary world.

Nevertheless, the academic session of 1967-1968 was a wonderful time in my life. We had found temporary accommodation in a lovely old farmhouse at 110 Collingwood, and George Whalley and the English Department had been exceptionally welcoming. Indeed, George Whalley was himself an exceptional man.

Both by temperament and determination a Renaissance man, he had made contact with the National Film Board to find out about technology and had checked out the most suitable sites on campus for 16mm film. He had secured an equipment budget within the English Department and another for film rentals. He had passed my list of essential film books directly on to Larry Edmund's specialized bookshop in Los Angeles and had put things in motion to "borrow" from the Engineering Department the services of a technician who knew about film. All this before I arrived.

When I did arrive, George took me to meet the dean. "I understand you'll need money for film production," Dean Harrower said. Would \$25,000 be enough?" I couldn't believe my ears. But I was naïve. If I had explained that I really required \$125,000, in those days I would have got it.

During my first week in Kingston, Joan and I were invited to dinner by the principal. Not only did the wonderful J.A. Corry look like W.C. Fields, he was even funnier. He wanted us to meet his daughter who was interested in film, and one of his chief advisors who was also at dinner had worked for the CBC.

What a world I had stumbled into! With John Meisel aping Groucho Marx, with a principal that looked like W.C. Fields and with a dean who carried his head a bit to one side as if from watching too many Laurel and Hardy movies, Queen's seemed like the perfect place to set up a film department.

Initially, however, I was simply in charge of a film program within the English Department. I was asked to teach both an introductory course and a more specialized seminar. Because the introductory course was open to everyone, I decided to base it on Hollywood with special reference to cinematic genres like the Musical and the Western. The seminar, which Whalley had arranged as a credit course within the English Department, would deal with films from Europe and with the classic cinema of Japan. At the time, except for those Film Board documentaries, I knew little about Canadian film.

In those days, since film represented a challenging field of inquiry with no established discipline, one could organize courses in a variety of ways. One had to *imagine* different approaches to the material.

For instance, one year I organized my American course

completely around the Western. Since there were few serious texts of genre analysis, I planned it as a colonial history of the west. We started with Eastern seaboard films like *Northwest Passage* and *Drums Along the Mohawk*, moved west with the original *Cimmarron* (1931) and ended up in Montana with *The Far Country* and *The Hanging Tree*. I counterbalanced the mining violence in *The Hanging Tree* with *City of Gold*—a nostalgic depiction of the *absence* of violence during the Klondike gold rush in Canada. Bit by bit, I was referring to Canadian films.

As there was little written about Westerns that was specific to film, we studied Turner's frontier thesis and read Henry Nash Smith's *Virgin Land*. For their course assignments students could relate the representations found in the films to comparable representations in pulp literature or to historical speculation. Such a course was less concerned with disciplining the intelligence than with stimulating the imagination. It was wonderful. However, in order to gain respectability within academe and to secure graduate funding, film studies was soon to develop along more disciplinary lines. It would be impossible within a film studies program today to offer such a general course on the Western.

Although I wanted to establish filmmaking, I didn't want to teach production. I was scarcely qualified; but I knew enough to get things started. I also knew that some production experience is important in grounding students in the materiality of the medium they are studying.

To study film and never touch it is like learning a language and never speaking it. Furthermore, from a *humane* point of view, if you set out to make a film on a person or an event, you have to enter into some kind of human relationship with that person or event. This pedagogical position relates back to my belief, confirmed by working with Douglas Lowndes in London, that to be fulfilling, education should have both a practical and a theoretical component.

73

I had no trouble with this philosophy at Queen's; but as film studies has become more specialized, I have been unable to persuade the other institutions where I have worked seriously to consider such a position. At York University, theory was seen as an irrelevance for the production training program that was already in place; at Carleton, any kind of production has always seemed a threat to the conceptual purity of theory. The only place were these two components are still held in balance is at Queen's.

Wanting to make production available to the university community, with the most rudimentary equipment I founded Quarry Films. The first film we made was an 8mm study of the Santa Claus parade, utilizing three people on camera and another three on sound. After that there were a number of editors striving to paste it all together.

Although the final film was technically primitive, the collective activity was empowering. Everyone involved gained experience in capturing images and sounds and then in relating them to one another to form a statement on film.

Standard 8mm was a wonderful medium. In miniature, it parallelled professional 35mm. With one exception: there could be no synchronous sound. While this was felt as a disadvantage, pedagogically it was a blessing. With that primitive technology, a film of talking heads was impossible. It forced students to devise image/sound relationships in innovative ways.

Along with such 8mm "sketching" activities, occasionally we made a 16mm film. Again the camera we had—a fragile Beaulieu—could scarcely handle synch sound; and one of the surprises and, to this day, one of the delights is the fact that in the first few years, the two best films were made, not by film students, but by an economics and a medical student. You don't have to know a lot about film to make a movie. You have to have a good idea.

Furthermore, both *A One Two Many World*, by Richard

Swindon, and *Cabbages and Kings*, by Peter Duffy, became National Film Board co-productions. I took great pride in this achievement, to have been able to enter into co-production with Tom Daly, the man who had produced all those films that I had seen in England, which had made me want to return to Canada.

From the profits of the film screenings that I had set up in the evenings, we would make little sketches on 8mm film and then, at the end of the year, I would bring in a professional like Terance Macartney-Filgate to supervise the synch-sound shooting for a more ambitious endeavour. In this way, we made *Walk*, a film on the miles-for-millions hike that was an annual event in those days; and we made *Bieler*, a portrait of the painter André Bieler who had done so much for the art scene both in Kingston and in Canada.

Although *Bieler* eventually played on the CBC, none of these films was particularly distinguished. Nevertheless, they launched the careers of distinguished filmmakers like Peter Raymont and Brigitte Berman and, as an editor, Gord McClellan. Indeed, after I had left, the enterprising troika that went on to head up Atlantis Films, which is still the most successful film production house in Toronto, also passed through Queen's.

Throughout all these activities I was helped enormously by Harry, my technical assistant. What would I have done without Harry Oosten?

Harry was the technician whom Whalley had stolen from the Department of Engineering, in spite of protests from Arthur Brebner, then Chair of the department.

Harry had been a member of the Dutch Film Lige, the group that produced such famous impressionist filmmakers as Joris Ivens. Harry had also made his own black-&-white films on 9.5mm—an eccentric gauge in North America but one quite common for a time throughout Europe. For years, Harry had been photographing cracks in concrete for the engineers—a sad sequel to his original filmmaking career. My arrival in Kingston gave him a new lease on life.

He was such a hard worker and he never complained. He projected for all the classes and for the evening screenings as well. He serviced the equipment; and for the afternoon lectures, he would locate any number of extracts within the various feature films that we could then use to illustrate some point in our discussions.

In a very real way, Harry was the backbone of the program. When my life came crashing down around me, he was always there, silently supporting me. Harry was very much that man who was not passion's slave and I did, indeed, wear him in my heart's core. I shall never forget him.

Finally, as I have mentioned, I also set up a series of evening screenings. In effect, I founded a university cinémathèque.

These screenings were academically necessary, I explained to the authorities, to give interested students a chance to see important films again, after the class discussion; but I also arranged, somewhat in breach of my contract with the distributors, to open these screenings to the public.

Although, unfortunately, they contributed to the decline of the Kingston Film Society, the evening screenings were immensely successful. They played to packed houses twice a week in Ellis Hall and gave film a profile throughout the university that, on their own, a couple of courses could never have done.

Initially, I introduced every screening with a stand-up irreverence appropriate for the age of Mort Sahl, on whom I secretly modelled myself. I even provided simultaneous translation for a number of French films that were available from Quebec that I wanted to screen.

One of these was Luis Buñuel's *Le Journal d'une femme de chambre*, still an underknown film, that features Jeanne Moreau and Michel Piccoli.

The day of the screening arrived. I was very nervous. From

a French copy of the script, I had prepared a spartan translation for my voice-over commentary. We didn't have the equipment to do it professionally and while I was familiar with the process from screenings at the National Film Theatre in London, I was by no means a seasoned performer.

I introduced the film. I explained how the commentary would be rough. I went back into the projection booth where the meticulous Harry had everything ready for us—including the anamorphic lenses necessary to project a film in CinemaScope. The house lights dimmed and, after a shot of gulls in the sky that I didn't remember, on came the opening title—*Le Journal d'Anne Frank*. The distributor had sent the wrong film.

That's show-business! It happens all the time; and while I can't remember what we did for that particular screening, when we got the film for the following week, my voice-over worked well enough, and everyone enjoyed that remarkable film.

Another thing we did was to show silent films with specially arranged scores. Although we didn't have a pianist who could accompany films in the appropriate manner, through the Toronto Film Society I had gained access to sound tapes prepared with great care by a film *aficionado* who was then a producer at the CBC. He had "scored" a number of silent films for the TFS and agreed to rent me his tapes. While the cues were spotty and synchronization a nightmare, it was better than nothing. In the course of using these tapes, moreover, there was at least one moment of cinematic revelation.

Although I had written about him and certainly respected his energy and intelligence, Sergei Mikhalovich Eisenstein had never been one of my truly favourite filmmakers. Much of his work seemed too juvenile in imagination and too willed in execution. I knew it was important, but I never really cared about it. I particularly thought *The General Line* silly in the extreme. How could anyone take all that nonsense seriously—

making a film about the collectivization of agriculture?

Nevertheless, as a programmer, I was determined to show it. I had access to a sound tape and I thought I would see how it went.

It *was* a revelation. Listening to the sweeping strings of some symphony by Katchachurian over fields of symmetrical tractors snaking their way across the screen and then hearing a gaggle of balalaikas during the bull/cow mating scene, the poor animals dressed up with great mischief in typical wedding apparel, the audience roared with laughter. When the final, "silly," titles appeared at the end of this sequence—"Hooray for the Co-operative! Long live the Co-operative!"—the entire audience burst into applause.

There is nothing that I have read about Eisenstein that has given me a comparable insight into the possible intentions of this film which that sound tape, however randomly assembled, managed to provide. Everyone left the screening thinking they had seen a wonderful film. Indeed, they had.

There were a couple of other things we did which, again, I simply stumbled upon. One was a single event; the other determined the course of my life.

The Salvador Dali/Luis Buñuel co-production, *Un Chien Andalou* is also a silent film. Although Buñuel had supervised a "sonorized" version, I wasn't happy with it. First of all, a soundtrack required that we project it at the wrong speed; and, secondly, while Wagner's *Tristan and Isolde* was the appropriate "serious" music for this film, the *pasa doble* that had been chosen as "a popular tune of the day" (which was what Buñuel wanted) was not a popular tune of *our* day. I decided to give the film a more contemporary reference.

By running it silently for the first few minutes before bringing in the Wagner, we were certainly respecting Buñuel's intentions. Just before we cut to the lovers buried in the sand at the end, however, Harry faded down the Wagner and brought up a popular tune of our day—"All You Need Is

Love"! The audience was in stitches.

It was this kind of playful inventiveness that seemed so effortless at the time and which met with such approval that made me think that, at Queen's University, in Kingston, Ontario, in the nineteen-sixties, I could get away with anything.

Outside Ellis Hall, of course, this was not to be the case.

One final story about the evening screenings—the one that changed my life.

Encouraged by the attendance at French films for which I prepared a primitive translation, I wondered what would happen if I ran French material with no translation at all. After all, there was a substantial French department at the university and I had noticed French-speaking people (we didn't yet call them Francophones) about the town for whom there seemed to be no culture at all. Furthermore, through the resources of the cinémathèque at the French Embassy in Ottawa, always with the courteous help of Violette Fagenwinter, I could get a number of features free of charge.

The third year I was at Queen's, I ran a series called "Le Cinéma Français" showing films by Jean Renoir, Claude Chabrol, Jacques Demy, Agnès Varda, Alain Resnais, Chris Marker and Jean-Luc Godard that were available in Canada but with no English tiles. Since most of the films were free, it wouldn't matter if only a few people came. The French Department was delighted.

There were not just a few people. The place was packed. We were amazed. The largest constituency came from the Royal Military College. Half the college was francophone and, as I had noticed, there were no activities in French at all in Kingston at that time.

Encouraged by this success, I mounted a similar program the following year. This time it would be "Le Cinéma Canadien" (we were just beginning to say québécois). Helped enormously by a young woman then working at the National

79

Film Board in Toronto, a Franco-Albertan named Françoyse Picard, I managed to locate prints of all sorts of québécois material that the distribution people in Montreal didn't even know existed. Françoyse soon went on to become the film officer for the Canada Council where, throughout her twenty-year stay, she did more for independent film production in Canada than any other single person—an achievement that has never been sufficiently acknowledged.

It was through these screenings in Kingston, however, that I first became acquainted with the films of Pierre Perrault, Gilles Groulx, Gilles Carle, Claude Jutra and Jean Pierre Lefebvre. I came to recognize that there was a distinctive "art" cinema right next door in the nation-province of Quebec. It was through these screenings, therefore, that I began to slip sideways into the culturally nationalist position that would soon occupy the greater part of my life.

I became a one-man film institute. I designed forms for the booking of films; I travelled to Toronto to "do deals" with the film distributors; I made contact with the people responsible for all the other film programs in Ontario and even managed, prematurely as it worked out, to set up a national association; I sought out inexpensive filmmaking equipment; and for relaxation, we would go off with our friends to skinny dip in a variety of nearby lakes.

We also gave what we called "beautiful people" parties. After we had bought a little house further down on Collingwood, Joan and I did a lot of entertaining. Along with the Meisels, there were a couple of other couples whom we constantly saw. We did everything together and, generally on Friday nights, we had parties. Often a number of students would attend.

We were playing with fire; but I had no idea that many of us would get burned. I was so extravagant. Along with Richard Trousdel who taught for a few years in the Drama Department, I was the hottest thing on campus. And we knew it, Richard and I. When "celebrity" friends such as Eleanor Bron came to visit, I would take them to the Faculty Club and behave outrageously.

I even took students to the Faculty Club, something that was not then allowed. I would go there with Krista Maeots, to have serious discussions about the state of Canadian politics; and with the wonderful Ellie Epp, to discuss the nature of integrity and creation. The result of all this self-display is that when the sky fell in, I had no moral credit.

Although hubristic in what I was doing, I was trying to prove that I was now free from the repressions I had suffered during my summers at the Hermitage. I was trying to establish (although I never thought of it like this) that I was no longer dependent on the imagination of a woman to design my life for me: I was busy designing my own life. Except I wasn't. If I had really wanted to succeed in what I was doing, eventually to set up a new home with another woman and her children, I wouldn't have been socially so arrogant.

At the same time, the whole world was changing. Within the English Department at the time, everybody's marriage broke apart, up one side of the corridor and down the other. Serious social shifts were occurring that, finally, we were all part of. We thought we were actors, determining our fate. We were actually being acted upon.

The old social structures were giving way, releasing an increasing emphasis on the self. The flower generation was quickly to become what Christopher Lasch would call the "Me Generation" of the nineteen-seventies; and the nineteen-eighties would take us into the space of a terrible cynicism as the sense of endless wealth and ease began to disappear, leaving us floundering around within a solipsism so total in the nineteen-nineties that one scarcely notices it.

In the nineteen-sixties, however, few of us could have foreseen that the world was developing the kind of self-regarding, opportunistic social ethic that represents the current stage of capitalistic greed.

Nevertheless, amid the personal chaos there was the achievement in film. Setting the cultural priorities for film studies at Queen's University in Kingston is one of the finest things I have achieved—more than my books, more than all my other cultural activities. There is something in the Queen's achievement that has endured.

In this perpetually changing world, Queen's is the one place I can return to where I still experience traces of my former activities. There is nothing now in Toronto; there is nothing in London—not even a wisp of the old Education Department at the British Film Institute. But at Queen's, some initiatives remain.

For one thing, the department is still located on Stuart Street in the little houses (it was initially one house) that I fought so hard for. There is still a decent balance between theory and practice and a dedication across the board to the Canadian cinema.

Throughout the years, the department has been helped enormously by the number of distinguished scholars who have taught there and moved on.

When film studies was established as a separate department, the first thing I did was to invite Robin Wood to join me from England. Even then, he was one of the most prolific film critics writing in English, with books on directors as diverse as Alfred Hitchcock, Ingmar Bergman, Howard Hawks and Claude Chabrol. He has lived on to achieve an influence and longevity even greater than Pauline Kael.

Robin left his mark on the department by his personal seriousness and by the students that he influenced. Robin is the kind of teacher whose intensity creates disciples; and of course, his international critical achievement added enormously to the prestige of film studies at Queen's.

After Robin came Jim Kitses whose book, *Horizon's West*, was an important stucturalist study of the Western. Jim is responsible for introducing the study of experimental film to Queen's, still an important aspect of the department's curriculum.

Raymond Durgnat was there for a year, and then Peter Morris, *the* English-speaking historian of Canadian cinema. Peter was the person who most consolidated the Canadian offerings and began to establish a mini-archive on campus for Canadian film.

It is Bill Nichols, however, who turned the place upside down. By theorizing the basic thrust of the department, he transformed what was a dynamic yet still unfocused liberal arts program into one of the most conceptually demanding disciplines on campus. While his influence has subsided somewhat since he returned to the United States, the rigor remains. His influence was crucial, a fact never fully acknowledged—sometimes to the annoyance of Nichols himself.

I have never encountered before or since a teaching and learning environment comparable to that which I experienced at Queen's. While I have missed it enormously, I never regret having left. Had I not, Morris or Nichols might not have been appointed and the department would not be what it is today.

Kingston provided the symbolic fulfilment of my conditioning as a pseudo-gentleman. Although I didn't go to Ridley College, I did get to Cambridge and I did land a most prestigious appointment at Queen's University. My parents should have been proud of me. Of course they weren't.

Actually, they couldn't have cared less. They never much cared for anything I did. They never once visited me. If my mother still thought that I belonged to the world, my father probably thought that I was some kind of poof. After all, wasn't I involved in the arts? And didn't I wear my hair too long, almost touching my collar?

My father had no way of apprehending me. I was neither a doctor nor a lawyer and I wasn't a jock. I was just an irritation in his life, part of the cosmic failure of the world that didn't turn out the way his mother, Saint Elizabeth, had promised him it would.

My father had always been a simple man, a thoughtlessly

intolerant man; but in his final years he became a monster. He was now somewhere in his seventies and my mother in her late sixties and neither of them was well. They were both junkies. They drank and smoked all the time and took an increasing variety of pills. My father believed that there was a pill for everything—an inheritance that throughout my life I have been trying to shake off.

As my father approached retirement, they moved into a highrise on Jackes Avenue by Yonge and St. Clair in downtown Toronto. When we first returned to Canada in 1967, I took my family to visit them. They hadn't seen my kids in over five years. "You better lose some weight, fellow!" was the first thing my father said to my slightly overweight son; and he said something equally insulting to Jennifer. They never went back. They refused. They didn't even attend the funerals. Why should they? What were my parents to them? What were they to me, for that matter? At the same time, there is something in this situation that fills me with regret.

Although my father had marched back at the end of the war announcing that he had two years to live, twenty years later he continued to parade his imminent death. It was my mother, however, who was dying. I could see it in her look.

Her eyes were grey and distant, as if a film were passing over them, separating her vision from the actualities of the world. Having smoked all their lives, they both had emphysema. It was a contest between the two of them, who would go first, my father always claiming that he had priority.

I helped my mother get the jump on him. She had been very ill one winter and for a number of weeks had been in an oxygen tent. While I made several trips to see her as, indeed, did Barbara, since we both lived out-of-town it was my younger sister, Sparrow, who got saddled with the care.

At that time, Sparrow was an intensely unhappy young woman. She had every reason to despise my father and despise him she did. Yet she couldn't escape his hateful hold on her because she loved her mother. She was, as she had always been, paralyzed by this double bind.

My mother recovered from her illness and returned home "to look after Father," as she always said—a job that she was scarcely able to do. Sparrow assisted in whatever way she could. That was the winter of 1969. In the spring of 1970, after term was over, I was planning to spend six weeks in Quebec City improving my French. This was the second year of my divorce and my children were joining me to drive down to Rockport, to have the kind of holiday that kids have with their exiled fathers.

Just before I departed for Quebec, Sparrow telephoned in panic. Mother was ill again and she couldn't do it anymore: she couldn't go on looking after our parents. She said I couldn't go to Quebec. I had to do my share. I had to come to Toronto and look after Dad.

That was not the way I saw the matter. However, I agreed to visit Toronto before I went east—to settle things, one way or another. After all, they had enough money. Hired help could be obtained. There are ways of dealing with these problems that are not a perpetuation of domestic tyranny.

I had to deal with Mother. Although she had little more than a cold, since her lungs were so fragile they had shipped her into hospital just, as they said, to keep an eye on her. I had to talk tough. I had to free Sparrow from the slavery that was expected of her, a slavery that was invisible because so assumed.

My mother was a proud woman, perhaps a strong-willed woman. I never really knew. She was certainly proud of her western roots in Brandon, Manitoba, and loved to describe herself as "a little prairie flower, growing wilder by the hour." She also liked to say that she was the guy who put the salt in the ocean.

Visiting her in hospital that spring in 1970 before I went off to Quebec, man-like I laid down the law. I explained the situation, the unacknowledged servitude of my sister, the possibility of professional help, the need to let other people look after them. "Constance," I said—I had always called her Constance when I talked tough with her—"you can't do it anymore. You're no longer the guy who put the salt in the ocean."

My mother was furious. It was the first real confrontation we had had since my high-school years when, with teenage arrogance, I had given her a copy of Harry Overstreet's *The Mature Mind*, proclaiming that once she had read it, we could talk seriously for the first time!

Of course she never did. Why should she? And we never had that talk; but with her lying in hospital some twenty years later, we were having it now. "The trouble with you," she screamed back at me, "is that you always think you're right but I *know* I'm right."

I cannot remember what plans were agreed upon. I think arrangements were made that the woman who was looking after Dad while Mother was in hospital would continue when she went home. But she never went home.

During the second week of my course in Quebec, I got a call from my father. "Your mother has passed away," he said on the phone. It was my father's finest hour. At this time, as during the small ceremony that followed in a few days, my father was erect and dignified, a stoical Anglo-Saxon to the core. This is how he must have been during the two world wars. This is how he presented himself to other people. He was proud and restrained and totally under control. I had never before seen him with this degree of public dignity.

He said I needn't come to the funeral. He explained that it would be a small affair. He recognized that I had other things to do, that I belonged to the world. As always, I was being factored out of family intimacy. "Dad," I said, "I'll be there. Of course, I'll be there." And for a few minutes, we talked about other things.

In my jazz-band days when I used to hang about with the boys, we would occasionally talk about our families. Age was a credential. Whenever someone asked about my mother, in my determination to be hip I would say that she was as old as

Louis Armstrong. Both my mother and Ol' Satchmo had been born at the turn of the century.

There are times in one's life when coincidences are extraordinary. When I flew into Toronto for my mother's funeral, all the newspapers had the same headline: "Louis Armstrong Dead". If my mother and Louis Armstrong had been born in the same year, they died within days of each other.

It appears that after I had left the hospital, having in a real sense taken away her pride, my mother had turned to the wall and died. If she couldn't believe she was in charge of things, she didn't want to put up with them. In a sense, what she had done to Nellie Hogger I did to her.

I didn't plan it that way. At the time, I never even made the connection. But thinking about it now, a connection is there. While I still feel awkward, telling this story, I felt no remorse. It was time for her to go. Sparrow had to be free. At least now both of them were relieved from the tyranny of my father.

It took me a little longer to do in my dad. After his nobility at my mother's funeral, he became a raging man. "Goddammed selfish bitch," he actually screamed one day (I was visiting him regularly), "and I just bought her a self-winding watch!" Having lost his audience, however, there was no need for him to linger.

The last days of his life were like Tolstoy's Ivan Illyich. I tried to explain that to Sparrow, to help her understand. She couldn't go near him. If she did he screamed. What he lacked, however, was a peasant body to hoist his legs up onto his shoulders to grant him at least the temporary relief that Tolstoy's wounded burger had enjoyed.

It was New Years Eve when we let him pass away. I was with him in the hospital, talking to him, trying to explain as he ebbed in and out of consciousness, that I was his son.

Although I had ordered a cessation of transfusions, this perfunctory changing of blood that was keeping him alive, the doctor wanted one more test. Because it was New Year's Eve, they were short of staff. The doctor asked me to serve as orderly, to bend back my father's arm so his riddled veins would be available for one last hit.

After the blood was taken, I continued to hold my father's arm. While I sensed his great terror as he slipped into his final unconsciousness, I felt so sad—not at his imminent death but at the realization that this was the only time in my life that I had ever touched my father. It had never been allowed.

At his funeral, all kinds of people swarmed Barbara and me. What a fine man, your father was, all of them said. How thoughtful and self-sacrificing, how gentle and patient, how dignified and strong! It seems that, like Isak Borg in *Wild Strawberries*, my father was a wonderful man for people who had not been emotionally close to him. Perhaps in my life, I too have been the same.

The death was attributed to emphysema. They have to put something on the form. He also had cirrhosis although what he really died of was a defeat of the spirit.

The values he had fought for in two world wars had not been sustained. He had watched his world crumbling slowly away. But as Pee Wee Russell said about the death of Bix Biederbeck, the wonderful jazz cornetist who, supposedly, died of pneumonia: "Man, he didn' die a'va cold. He died a' everything." My father died of everything.

Six

1974 represents a watershed in my life. It initiated the final division between a life with my family and a life on my own, between Queen's University at Kingston and York University in Toronto.

It also marked the end of the professional ties I once had with the British Film Institute in London. 1974 witnessed serious ideological shifts both in my domestic and in my professional life.

It was my first sabbatical. What an extraordinary feeling—a year's leave on full pay to do whatever I wished! I had received a grant from the Social Sciences and Humanities Council to put the finishing touches on what was to be my *magnus opus*—my critical study of the films of Eisenstein, Renoir, Bergman, Buñuel, Fellini and Godard. Originally, there were to have been eight directors, including Antonioni and Resnais; but for reasons of cost, we had decided to restrict my study to six. The book was also to contain an extended introduction that I felt at the time would elevate film criticism on to another level. This elevation, of course, never occurred.

By the time of my sabbatical, however, *Six European Directors* had been over a year in page proof. My desire to be in London was more to catch up with the new things that were happening in European theory, developments that I had had to keep at bay while struggling through the chaos of divorce to finish my book.

I had all but abandoned it. There had been too many distractions. Furthermore, I knew that the tone of film writing was changing and that a thoughtful but not an academic book was soon to be entirely out-of-date. Had it not been for the encouragement of Paul Schrader, at that time the editor of *Cinema*, a California journal, I might never had finished it. By insisting that I review Ingmar Bergman's *A Passion* when, during the summer of 1971, I was working for the American Film Institute in California, he got me writing again.

The film blew me away. I hadn't been so affected in the cinema since I had seen Fellini's *La Dolce Vita* in 1959. Not only is *A Passion* formally one of the most balanced films that Bergman has ever made, but I identified totally both with Andreas Winkelman and with the social situation of violence, pain and defeat. How well I understood his need to retreat from the torments of life back into solitude, to crawl away into loneliness—into *ensamhet*—one of Bergman's favourite words. It seemed perfectly to parallel my own situation.

While I was already divorced, the woman for whom I had abandoned my family was about to abandon me. With the help of all our former friends, her husband had kidnapped their children. It was a horrendously destructive situation. Indeed, experiencing Bergman's film seemed like a bit of relief. It was not only *my* life, I could then assure myself, that was so pointlesly destructive.

In 1974, however, when returning to England, I had decided to affiliate myself to the film program at the Slade School of Fine Art at the University of London. I wanted to find out what was happening in the film scene in Great Britain.

I knew that changes in critical priorities had taken place but I didn't realize that a reign of terror had begun. Although the student uprisings in Paris in May 1968 had happened six years previously, the ideological battles were still raging amongst the intelligentsia in the London of 1974.

What the new Turks were attacking was, in essence, humanism. They railed against "bourgeois ideology" as something that had to be destroyed. Re-reading Marx through Louis Althusser and Freud through Jacques Lacan, they declared themselves in favour of a "science" of knowledge and against the "impressionistic relativism" of an earlier age. In Stuart Hall's classic description of this period as a shift between an empirical and a theoretical paradigm, he doesn't mention that it was also a shift from a British to a French tradition.

As an acculturated colonial who had gained access to the British tradition through luck and hard work, I couldn't understand why everyone was against it. What about the Great Tradition? How can there be culture without continuity? How can one proceed with reformation through amputation? My cries of outrage fell upon plugged ears.

Central to this theoretical discourse were two left-wing journals—*The New Left Review* and the film magazine *Screen*. Begun at the time of the Suez crisis in the nineteen-fifties and edited for years by Stuart Hall, *The New Left Review*, when taken over by Perry Anderson, reflected the influence of Parisian theory; and shortly afterwards, when Sam Rhodie took over *Screen*, he transformed it from a teachers' manual into the most prestigious film journal in English that the world has ever seen.

A number of people were associated with these journals. If I single out Ben Brewster it is because, through his extremely literal translations from the French of the works of Louis Althusser, he created the jargon that was to dominate film studies for the next fifteen years. It represented, indeed, a most significant intervention into the current problematic! Shy film academic and part-time theorist, Brewster may have had a greater effect on the English language than any other writer since Shakespeare.

Chief guru at the Slade during the year I was there was Noël Burch. An American from Oakland, he had come to Europe the same time I had; but he had gone to France while I went to England. We both knew a lot about film but from conflicting perspectives. We immediately hated one another.

For Burch, since everything around him spoke bourgeois ideology, everything was wrong. One time, fed up with the lack of rigor among the students at the Slade, he assigned Foucault's *Archaeology of Knowledge* to be read over the Christmas break.

But this was a film seminar! Why weren't we talking about films? When we returned to the theoretical brainwashing sessions disguised as film seminars in January, no-one in the class had anything to say. It was like my days at Cambridge only worse: I wasn't learning anything—except about human nature.

"Well," said I, trying to be helpful, "Foucault seems to

hover on the brink of an epistemological agnosticism. We can't know anything directly—only through the mediation of cultural texts." Everybody looked at me in collective embarrassment. Burch looked at me with fury. How dare I speak if I didn't know the correct thing to say? Well I didn't so I did.

To this day, that doesn't seem to me to have been a stupid thing to say. If Burch had returned with What do you mean? Give me an example, we might have had a discussion. As it was, he simply declared this English-speaking group not up to his Parisian theoretical standards and, because we were collectively such dolts, we would have to look at films.

Even then, there were problems. He would sit with a given film on an editing table, stopping and starting it, supposedly inquiring about the meaning of images but actually deciding what he wanted us to say.

I remember one time he was presenting *Hiroshima, Mon Amour*. If ever there is an example of "bourgeois aesthetics," surely it is to be found in the films of Alain Resnais—with a different subject of address, of course, than the films of François Truffaut but within a similar aesthetic space nevertheless.

Not so for Burch. Because the film addressed the bomb and contested the dominant codes of filmic narrative, it was radical. Being on the left, it was on the right side.

One day, as he was spinning through a particular sequence on his way to affirming an ideological assertion, he was talking about the different ways of linking shots when he said, "For our purposes, a dissolve can be considered the same as a cut." "Noël," I said, still trying to be helpful, "a dissolve is *not* the same as a cut." I went on to talk about what in the post-theoretical age we might call the different semantic potential of the dissolve and the cut—perhaps even the different ideological implications, since Truffaut is all dissolves and Godard all cuts.

Everyone looked at me as if the ass had spoken. The bourgeois aesthete had one again brayed. It didn't matter that what I said was true. Truth was not a value within the Slade School of Fine Arts in 1974. "Correctness" was what counted.

I think I should have gone out of my mind that year had it not been for one woman. She became my private tutor. However it happened, we became friends.

Being from the poshest of posh backgrounds, with a g-dropping accent that made the Queen herself sound common, she probably recognized that this theoretical discourse, for all its assertions of political utility, was simply the current academic game. In a few years, such an attitude would imply, we would all be playing a different game. In effect, she was wiser than I. Her name was Kari Hanet.

Being fluent in French, she played the game well. Basically she served as a teaching assistant to Burch. When they were alone together, he always spoke French with her, as if to demonstrate that it was easier to be ideologically correct in a foreign language.

Kari was engaged to Paul, a medical student whom I never really knew. It was a combination of his busyness and my passionate unhappiness that brought Kari and me together; but very quickly we started going out together, seeing films together, having meals together.

She led me hand-in-hand through Roland Barthes' *Elements of Semiology* and *Writing Degree Zero*, telling me what they were doing, explaining why Barthes was important. In fact, though only recently translated, these texts had been written in the nineteen-fifties.

All that I understood. In a country where standards for the French language and culture are imposed by the *Acadamie Française*, of course it is necessary to challenge that authority. In a language that narrates its history in an unchallengeable mode of address known as *le passé defini*, it is understandable— that longing for a zero degree of writing, even though such a longing is impossible of fulfilment. Whatever our desires,

93

there is no escape from, in Fredric Jameson's phrase, the prison-house of language.

Except that in English, the entire cultural surround is different. There has never been an *Acadamie Anglaise*, and the English language has always been more welcoming to emerging vernaculars, from classic cockney to contemporary rap. But these differences were not talked about at the Slade. English bad, French good constituted the dominant pedagogy of that time.

One day in February, *Six European Directors* appeared. It was the source both of enormous pride and of considerable embarrassment.

There can be no greater thrill for writers than to walk about the streets of London, past their favourite bookshops in which, in the past, they have purchased books and then, one day, to see their own book sometimes filling an entire window. There was no advance press and no official launching; but England was still England. It was a literate society and I was, I believe, the last of the Pelican originals. Not only had I almost not finished the book, but by the time I did, it almost hadn't come out.

Between the commissioning of the work and the delivery of the copy, the directors at Penguin had completely changed their policy. Having been badly burned commercially by a series of texts they had published for the Open University— including Brewster's translations of Althusser—Penguin had decided to get out of commissioning books and into the lucrative business of paperback rights for bestsellers and established classics. In England, to a large extent, this is what they are still doing today.

My book, however, belonged to a former time. Commissioned by a wonderful editor, Nikos Stangos, it was designed as a companion piece to V.F. Perkins' *Film as Film*— Victor dealing with the popular Hollywood film and I with the art cinema of Europe. They were both seen as sequels to Penelope Houston's *The Contemporary Cinema*.

94

By the time *Six European Directors* appeared, however, Nikos had left Penguin and any dynamic interest in my book had disappeared. It was published as a kind of alimony. I had been under contract for so long.

While the reviews were generally favourable, it was still embarrassing, having the book come out at that time. With its naïve insistence on the value of "response" as a critical universal, *Six European Directors* was completely at odds with the deconstruction of the very notion of universality by all the political theory circulating at the Slade. My book embodied everything the new discourse was against.

One day I arrived at the Slade to find three of my young colleagues, each with his own copy, engaged in a mock preoccupation of examining it studiously. They weren't being nasty: it was just a tease; but I heard that my friend Kari Hanet had said that from *Six European Directors* she had learned more about me than she had about the cinema. For the sake of friendship I had to challenge her.

Brilliant though she was, Kari had published only one article. She had placed in *Screen* a semiological discussion of *Hiroshima, Mon Amour*—an article that had earned the praise of the chief guru in Paris at that time, Christian Metz. It was a good piece, intricate and elegant—far more accessible than many articles in *Screen*.

When I arrived at her place for one of our dates, I asked her about my book. Yes, she admitted, she had said what I had been told she had said. I decided to bargain with her. "Would you concede, Kari, when reading *Six European Directors* that you learned *as much* about me as you did about cinema?" She agreed that that might be a more accurate way of putting it. "Well," said I, "when I read your piece on *Hiroshima, Mon Amour*, I learned *as much* about semiology as I did about the film." "*Nous sommes quits*," she replied with a smile, offering me a kiss on the cheek as we set off on our date. We never mentioned the matter again.

From this story an observation follows. While I have no wish to be simplistically reductive, one of the differences between the old criticism and the new has to do with the position of the self within the text.

In "impressionistic" criticism, the self is always a part of the argument. Whether through the Leavisian invocation of peer discussion—"This is so, isn't it?"—or the often chatty way that Pauline Kael talks about the lifestyle of her friends when she is discussing a particular film, we can infer a sense of a personal presence, of someone whose mind we are getting to know. Indeed, a vitalist like D.H. Lawrence would assert that only an insightful person would have sufficient courage to be able to write illuminating criticism.

In "theoretical" criticism, on the other hand, the self is disguised. As if in imitation of scientific method, what is presented is a concern with system. After the reign of terror of the nineteen-seventies and early nineteen-eighties, however, a dialogue between these two approaches is both possible and necessary. Indeed, it is already taking place.

Now that the dust has settled and the smoke has cleared, the battles have usefully altered the landscape of cultural practice. Certain positions have been surrendered and others have been gained. Painful though all these changes were for me at the time, I can now see that even the nastiness was part of a series of crucial shifts that were taking place in the western world.

Although we didn't yet know it, what was happening was the beginning of an accumulated challenge to the Eurocentric, androcentric, normative modes of cultural thinking. The tradition of European culture from the Greeks to T.S. Eliot, nearly all of it constructed by men, that idealist tradition which for Matthew Arnold constituted the treasure trove of "the best that has been thought and said in the world," that tradition was increasingly under attack. The semiological/structuralist intervention represented the first wave of cultural critics who were determined to find fresh ways of thinking about the world.

Moreover, whatever the excesses, there can now be no return to the humanistic confidence of the former Arnoldian position. That confidence was the result of a belief in a unified universe and in the superiority of the white patrician voice within it. With different cultures and different genders making their demands, that old-fashioned confidence has passed away. Voices are emerging from all over the world—women's voices, aboriginal voices—that are altering the conceptual landscape within which we live.

Following the "bourgeois" success of *Six European Directors*, I was asked by Studio Vista to write a short book on the French New Wave—on Chabrol, Truffaut, Godard and *toute cette gang* originally associated with *Cahiers du Cinéma*. It was to be a coffee-table book, with lots of lovely pictures but with a literate text—thereby targeting two "niche markets" at a time, as we would say nowadays.

That commission would constitute an unhappy event in my life. As with my Penguin, by the time this manuscript was delivered, in the space of eighteen months, the woman who had commissioned the work had left and the publishing policy had changed.

Studio Vista liked the pictures but no longer cared about the text. Then when James Monaco's book appeared in the United States on exactly the same clutch of directors, my project was dead. While I managed to place some chapters in a number of journals, I felt I knew a little—as much as a man can—about what it is like to experience a miscarriage.

When in England in 1974, the film department at York University had twice invited me to join them. I didn't want to go to York but the idea of leaving Kingston for Toronto was appealing.

Since my arrogant flouting of the received conventions of polite society had cost me in one year both my wife and my loved one, I felt extremely isolated in Kingston. There were no more Friday parties. There was no longer a vibrant social scene. Once again, I had pissed in my bed and the soiled mattress had been held up for all to see.

It was time to move on. I decided to take over the responsibility of my children, to accept a job at York and move them out of Kingston.

I cut short my year in London to return to Canada—to find a place to live with two fully grown teenagers in the city of Toronto. It was my chance to begin again—both as parent and person. This time, I would make everything work.

It was quite a production—accepting a job at York and finding a place to live and schools for my kids, because my son refused to go to an ordinary school. "Free" schools were all the rage; and eventually I found one for each of them that cost me an arm and a leg. I also found a house.

I don't know how I did it. On the day before the school term started we all moved into a wonderfully adequate space at what was then 45 MacPherson Avenue to start our new life in the big city. I felt as if I had just won two world wars.

Life at York was very different from life at Queen's. The pedagogical priorities were reversed.

Since Queen's is extremely privileged, the challenge was to animate the frequently overly civilized students who would attend such a prestigious university. At York, which in the nineteen-seventies, was still getting started, the challenge was to civilize barbarians. It was a task that my educational experiences in England had well prepared me for.

Actually, my first taste of York had occurred in London. I had been hired by telephone, first by John Katz who had just been appointed Chair, and then by Dean Joe Green who haggled about my salary. They were both, of course, Americans. Doing deals on the phone in this way, I felt I was moving to Texas!

Since Dean Green was coming to London, we arranged to meet at the BFI. I shall never forget that first encounter.

Coming down the stairs from the old library at 81 Dean Street, an appropriate location for this meeting, I couldn't believe my eyes. Here was this guy, the Dean of Fine Arts at York University, looking like the classic cliché of the American in Europe—plaid trousers, blue blazer, ascot and shades. We shook hands and went for a drink. I took him to a pub where I wouldn't be recognized.

I plunked a copy of *Six European Directors* on the table for his inspection. "Just so you'll know who you've hired," I said. When he asked me what I had been doing, I explained that I had been trying to come to grips with the challenge of semiology. "What d'hell is that?" asked Dean Green. At first I fumbled but then explained that it involved a systematic examination of the ideological implications of cultural signs. "Jesus," said Dean Green. "If you talk that way at York, the kids are gonna go bananas!"

So I knew what I was getting into. Set up by a young Californian by the name of Mark Rosen, the Film Department had been presided over during the previous few years by the most gentlemanly of gentlemen, the most graciously loquacious man I have ever met. James Beveridge was a product of the National Film Board. A contemporary of Tom Daly, Jim had spent a lot of time in India and then working in places like New York University.

Jim was a filmmaker of the old "aristocratic" school. He didn't believe that directors should get too bogged down with the nitty-gritty of actually shooting or editing a film. The "workers" did that for you. You gave the instructions and then took the credit.

This way of thinking was not the best preparation for supervising a film department. Furthermore, the priorities at York were very much for production over theory and the standards were derived from Hollywood. There was no reference to Canada at all.

The upshot for me was an increased focus upon an indigenous priority—increasingly, on the whole state of Canada as a nation. If in England films from the Film Board had made me want to return home, the American surround of so many of the priorities at York made me determined to clarify what it was to be Canadian.

Curiously enough, it was not until I went to York that I actually taught Canadian film. At that time, the first term of the introductory course dealt with Hollywood and the second with foreign cinema. I introduced Canadian films under the rubric of foreign cinema.

It worked well. After students had seen *Rome, Open City* and *Bicycle Thieves*, they had no trouble appreciating *Goin' Down the Road* or *Mon Oncle Antoine*. When I realized that substantially different discussions could be generated by screening Canadian films, I began to take more seriously the pedagogic potentialities of working with our own cinema.

The most important step in the development of my brilliant career as a Canadian nationalist occurred through my friendship with David Helwig. 1974 also marked the beginning of four fine years of CBC drama, with John Hirsch mandated to develop a wide range of dramatic programming. He was concerned both with popular sitcoms like "The King of Kensington" and with the traditionally more serious, Sunday night fare such as the "For the Record" series.

David had been offered the job of dramaturge—an offer he couldn't refuse. Still based in Kingston, he commuted to Toronto and had found a place to stay on MacPherson Avenue. In the evenings, he would drop in for a beer. We would talk about many things and I would blather on about my American life at York, about the hegemonic control of Hollywood over our film theatres and about many other things that were wrong with the world.

While David was sympathetic, he explained that it was no use railing at him: I had to find a public forum. It was through these encounters that he got me reviewing for *Books in Canada*. One of the first books I dealt with was Robert Fulford's anthology of his film columns from *Saturday Night—Marshall Delaney at the Movies.*

I said some nice things. I certainly praised the pellucidity of the prose. But I was writing a review. I wasn't going to be soft.

Basically, I complained that the book lacked focus and a consistent point-of-view. I believe I ended with the suggestion that what we really needed was not a collection of disparate articles but a book that, with greater rigor and consistency, would think through the problems of cinema—especially the problems of Canadian cinema.

The day my review appeared, I received a phone call from a woman at the CBC. She asked me if I would like to think through these problems for radio, as a series for "Ideas." With characteristic grace, I exploded: "Do a film series for radio? That's like doing television shows for the blind!" This was nonsense, of course. In England I had done a lot of work about film on radio. We talked some more and she persuaded me to come and see her. She again gave me her name, adding: "And just in case someone else tells you, I'm Robert Fulford's wife."

It was Geraldine Sherman who at that time was the executive producer for "Ideas." She was prepared to hire me for having insulted her husband in print! I thought that was marvellous.

From that initial contact followed a series of eight hours of radio on national cinemas, with Canada as important as any other country. From that series also followed a number of other commissions and, later on, another four-hour series. Throughout this time, working with Geraldine Sherman has been the happiest and most creative relationship I have known in my life.

Struggling with the first series which we called *Movies & Mythologies* was particularly rewarding. It was also enormously demanding. There wasn't much time.

Although I worked a good deal with archival material and had commissioned two friends to do my Canadian interviews while I flew off to London and Paris to acquire the European voices that I needed for the shows, I was faced with a frantic schedule. I felt like Charles Dickens—not knowing as I worked whether or not I would let Little Nell die.

And there was York; and John and Jenny—two very difficult teenage children! It was at this time that I began to spin out of control.

As I recount this period of my life, I like to make a joke of it. I had begun to make a joke about everything.

I claimed that I learned three things from the CBC: to work quickly, to write clearly and to drink before noon. In Toronto, with the pressures of York, my children and the CBC, I began to drink to work—to find both the energy and the ideas to do all the things I had to do.

Although surrounded by people, I felt increasingly alone. Occasionally a friend would come for tea and stay for breakfast, but I never managed to establish a peer relationship with a woman. Probably the drinking got in the way. Possibly having the kids about didn't help. I don't really know; but I do know that I felt myself falling into a state of hectically preoccupied loneliness.

After it was broadcast, *Movies & Mythologies* had a second life as a book of which I am very proud. Indeed, it has just acquired a third life in Japanese, published by Koyo Shobo in Kyoto.

Robbed of all the music tracks and voices, it is a funny book in a way—rather thin in terms of ideas; but in a country in which there were some filmic literacy, it could have served as an introductory text for high school students, giving Canada its place within the cinematic system.

"Peter makes all those filmmakers sound like heroes," Robert Fulford said to his wife when he heard the shows on the air. Heroes they were, in my view—striving to create a cinema in this country with almost no acclaim. If the politics of international publishing had extinguished my book on the French

New Wave, the politics of Canadian nationalism had given me a most comforting compensation and had begun to direct my attentions more securely toward the Canadian scene.

It was also during this time that the Toronto film festival got started—christened with characteristic understatement the "Festival of Festivals." It began as a modest affair, however, involving only four screens in two cinemas. The first year imported Jan Dawson from the BFI in England to introduce Torontonians to the New German Cinema—all those Fassbinder, Herzog, Wenders and Kluge films that were not yet known in Canada.

It was wonderful—a "new" new wave of films. Furthermore, seeing the films in their technical simplicity and learning about the politics of their production inspired me to analyze the ways in which in Canada we might achieve similar things.

For the second year of the Toronto film festival, instead of importing Jan Dawson, they hired me. Linda Beath had been brought on board by Bill Marshall and Hank van der Kolke, the founders of the festival, to co-ordinate the programming. Linda asked me to do some "specialty" programming—a role that I continued to play until the establishment of the Ontario Cinematheque rendered such programming redundant.

For the second year, however, I organized a mini-retrospective of the films of Max Ophüls—the most bittersweet romantic film stylist the world has ever seen. Very much to the surprise of Bill Marshall, who thought I was too academic to be an effective programmer, it was an enormous success.

Actually, I handled it well. As at Queen's, I introduced the films; the stand-up comedian came into play; I got written up in the newspapers; I even produced Peter Ustinov for one of the sceenings in which he had appeared; and at the end, I chaired a discussion on the value of the work with the participation of international scholars like Robin Wood.

Although I was gradually losing control of my life, those four years in Toronto were extremely productive. I was composing the first *auteur* studies of fine Canadian filmmakers such as Don Shebib, Allan King and Pierre Perrault for *Cinema Canada*; I did occasional film reviews for the CBC and book reviews for *Books in Canada*; I prepared a regular column on film for the *Canadian Forum*; I taught at York, and I really worked hard at running the house for my kids.

I cooked and cleaned and scrubbed and polished while the kids, of course, did nothing at all. They would have been happier had I done less. It would have made them feel more at ease.

I did it all. I saved the bones from the roasts to make nutritious soups. I set off for the St. Lawrence market on Saturday mornings to get the best buys. I carved kidneys into the shape of mushrooms so that Jen would swallow them without knowing what they were. I disguised spinach as lettuce; watermelon as tomatoes. I learned all the tricks of the homemaking trade.

They didn't do a thing. Jen claimed that since she was a feminist she didn't have to and John seemed not to notice. He never offered to shovel snow or do any of the other jobs that boys are expected to do. I didn't know how to ask him. I wanted him to volunteer.

Although Jen and I were somewhat distant from one another during her teenage years, I have never felt closer to my son. We would watch television together and I would massage his neck as if for stiffness but really, I think, so we could touch. While he smoked more grass than I would have wished, I couldn't assume a moral stance because I was drinking all the time.

We did talk, however—about the spaces one is fleeing from with the help of narcotics, about the spaces one is entering, the things that one is trying to do. I like to think that these talks were some help to him when he finally kicked the habit. It has taken me much longer to begin to kick mine.

When I was still at Queen's, I had been approached by Chris Faulkner of Carleton University. He was interested in setting up a film program within the English department in the way I had set up the program at Queen's. I was invited up to talk to them.

Presumably the meeting was productive because, bit by bit, they went ahead and designed what was the most carefully thought out program I had ever seen. I also think I was helpful in encouraging them not to think in terms of bringing in someone to get things going but in starting it themselves.

Nevertheless, after they had expanded sufficiently to make one or two junior appointments, Chris wanted a senior scholar such as I had become to help establish an honours program. By this time, John had finished school, Jen had enrolled in a fashion program at Dawson College and her Kingston boyfriend wanted to come to live with her in Toronto. I felt my work as a mothering father had come to an end.

Although I had been invited to Carleton for a visiting appointment of only one year, once again I wanted to burn my bridges. I wanted to leap over a cliff. With my characteristic efficiency, within the space of two weeks, I had found a place to live for my son; another for my daughter with her boyfriend; I had sold up my house and was off to chilly Ottawa.

I was setting out for yet another world. It would take me a couple of years to realize just how chilly Ottawa could be.

Seven

When I moved to Ottawa in 1978, the city seemed like a Paris of the north. The Canadian Film Institute was experiencing its glory days—the only glory days it has ever seen. Under the buccaneer directorship of Frederick Manter, cultural activists like Piers Handling and Wayne Clarkson were developing both the film screening and publication programs. The *Ottawa Review*, an intellectual tabloid, offered sensitive coverage of the arts in both our official languages; and as well as the National Arts Centre, there were five little theatres in town.

At the university, along with Film Studies, Carleton boasted an Institute of Canadian Studies that welcomed my Canadian film courses as a useful addition to their graduate program. As I was new and prestigious, everyone was welcoming. There was an excitement in the air. It was a bit like being back at Queen's.

There was also a latent energy, awaiting my arrival. Two graduate students in Canadian Studies, Steve Bingham and John Sharkey, were both film buffs and political nationalists. They formed the Canadian Film Group that, with the support of Françoyse Picard at the Canada Council, soon invited Canadian filmmakers to town to present their work on Friday evenings at Carleton University. All the parties were held at my place.

They were really exciting times, those first two years in Ottawa. The Trudeau Liberals were still in power and there was a lot of money around. Little did I know when I resigned from York that within a few months, everything would collapse. Handling, Clarkson, Bingham and Sharkey, along with other active members of the Ottawa film scene such as Joyce Mason, Sue McKenna, Michèle Maheux and later, Geoff Pevere, would all move to Toronto, leaving (as I am fond of saying nowadays) Uncle Peter behind!

Initially, however, in much of the work I did, I remained based in Toronto. I still prepared items for the CBC and in 1980 I began the busiest year of my life.

By that time, Wayne Clarkson had already moved to Toronto to take charge of the Toronto film festival. He wanted me to do something big.

Since Jean-Luc Godard was staging a theatrical come-back with *Sauve qui peut(la vie)*, we decided to do a massive Godard retrospective. Not only would we show all the Godard films but also some films that had influenced him and others that he had influenced—including some Canadian films. With five screenings a day for ten days, it was an enormous project.

I wasn't sure I was up to it. The Godard films, yes; but the American stuff? And all those films that came before?

Actually, it was easy. From Godard's own film reviews a wealth of material leapt out at me. Speaking about Jean Seberg in *À Bout de souffle*, Godard once explained that it was just *Bonjour Tristesse* three years later. So that is how we planned it. At 11.30 one morning we ran *Bonjour Tristesse* followed at 1.30 by *À Bout de souffle*. And we surrounded Godard's *Vivre sa vie* with *Abschied von Gestern* by Alexander Kluge and *Le chat dans le sac* by Gilles Groulx—two films that salute it. For those enthusiasts that were able to see the entire program—and there were many of them, virtually filling the Bloor cinema for each event—the retrospective was a revelation.

Unfortunately for me, it was a revelation in another way. Although beginning to do big things, the Toronto film festival was still a little festival and was seriously understaffed. Working with Wayne Clarkson, Anne Mackenzie was in charge of all the film bookings and, for my program at least, she was always half a day behind. Worse than that: in those days, every frame had to be approved by the Ontario Board of Film Censors, then headed up by the formidable Mary Brown.

It was a nightmare. No sooner did I get one film on the screen than I had to rush back to the Park Plaza either to locate the next film or to negotiate the censor's approval. Some films arrived in the nick of time; others didn't arrive at all. Some had never been booked. That is how it was in those days. The Toronto festival was soon to become the nine-ring circus that it is today and I guess the Godard retrospective helped it on its way.

For reasons of prestige, we wanted Godard to appear. Securing his phone number from Richard Roud in London, I began phoning him in Switzerland, writing him letters and then phoning him again. No firm plans emerged. What was Canada let alone Peter Harcourt to Jean-Luc Godard, even though we had met once or twice at events in the past.

Finally the agents entered the negotiations—Tom Luddy of Zoetrope who was handling the new film. To come for the opening at Toronto's "Festival of Festivals" Godard wanted one thousand American dollars in cash. My Canadian soul was outraged. I refused to do it. I wouldn't be the carrier of the filthy American lucre!

In the end, of course, I was. But everything else I did in my own way. Refusing the proffered limousine, I set off with my friend Joyce Mason to pick him up in my rusty Volkswagen, a decision that was written up in two of the Toronto newspapers. "Avant-garde filmmaker met by off-beat car," wrote the *Sun*—or words to that effect.

Apart from his appearance after the evening screening, I wanted to protect Godard from the press. I smuggled him off with some friends to a small French restaurant in the Annex, at which he ordered in English while the rest of us ordered in French. We entertained him with stories and basically helped him to rest, to get ready for the moment when he would have to go on stage. But with a nose for matters of publicity, Roger Ibert from Chicago had managed to insinuate himself.

With his pad and pencil at the ready, coveting his exclusive interview, Roger kept waiting for the appropriate moment. It never arrived. We saw to that. Toward the end of the dinner, however, he did manage one question.

He wanted to talk about *Weekend*—Godard's Swiftian analysis of the cannibalistic characteristics of consumer society. He mentioned the $350°$ circular tracking shot that choreographs the farmyard recital toward the end of the film, moving first in one direction, then in another, and finally, just for a moment, back in the first direction again. "I love that moment," Roger cooed. "It always gives me great pleasure. But why did you do it? Why did you move the camera back again?" "Perhaps dhat ees why I dheed eet," Jean-Luc replied, "To geeve a leetle pleazuh to peeple in Chicago."

Although the retrospective was an enormous success, it exhausted me. I was gulping down booze to give me energy and then popping pills to calm me down. "It's showtime, folks!" I would exclaim in the mornings, wiping away tears of fatigue. It is no wonder that when it came out, *All That Jazz* had such an effect upon me.

I habitually woke up crying. When by an accident, all the films were in place and I could let myself sit in the theatre, I found myself crying through most of the film. I was already in trouble but didn't know it. I just kept going. On to the next thing.

I returned from Toronto not only with my courses to teach (I don't know how I taught in those days) but also with seventeen québécois features awaiting my analysis. I had agreed to write a book on the films of Jean Pierre Lefebvre.

Although Clarkson had fled, Handling was still at the CFI and Bingham and Sharkey had joined him. They were organizing a retrospective of Lefebvre's works to tour across Canada—screenings largely to be held at the film co-operatives that Françoyse Picard and Joyce Mason had brought together as a national organization the previous year. It was to be a properly curated event and I had agreed to write the text.

Many of the films were without subtitles and my grasp of spoken French is far from perfect. How did I have the nerve to take on such a project? How did I have the gall to take on the many things that I did in those days?

As I went through the films, however, meanings began to emerge. Lefebvre's films create a universe. They are full of innovative structures and intense personal feelings.

Lefebvre very much cares about the state of the world. If his best films have the formal authority of Alain Resnais, they also possess the compassion of Jean Renoir. To this day I cannot understand why they are not more celebrated within our own country and throughout the world. They are probably too genuine, too sincere, too unique. They are both engaged and naïve. They are uncool. They are not smartly superior to everything they depict. They are increasingly out-of-step with the times in which we live.

If the Godard retrospective was an illustrious event, the Lefebvre retrospective was a love affair. It was a voyage both of discovery and of self-discovery. It was also a journey toward trust—a reciprocal trust between Jean Pierre and myself. It provided me with one of the most inwardly rewarding experiences of my life.

I wrote the book in three months. Indeed, returning from Toronto in September, I had a draft by the end of October.

Tumbling into my still rusty Volkswagen with my friend Barbara and her son Colin, I drove down to the Eastern Townships to spend a weekend with the Lefebvres, during which Jean Pierre and myself would prepare an extensive interview for the book.

We were all excited by the project—an excitement intensified by a most lovely Indian Summer weekend. While I didn't really know them well—I scarcely knew Marguerite at all and had never met their son Blaise—I knew them intimately through their films.

The weekend was a celebration—of film, friendship and the possibilities of nationhood. While Jean Pierre is very much a Québécois, he also recognizes that Quebec is part of Canada, which is in turn part of North America. Although I think being anglophone helped me to perceive recurring patterns in his work, Jean Pierre has never made me feel a foreigner, even though I come from away.

With the assistance of Piers Handling, the book was ready by February. We launched the retrospective in Ottawa with parties, both large and small, at my house.

We kicked off with *Il ne faut pas mourir pour ça* and *Le vieux pays où Rimbaud est mort*—the first two films of a projected trilogy made respectively in 1965 and 1971. They both feature Michel Sabourin as the detached, inquiring Québécois, and Michel came down for the event.

The Lefebvre launching was the antipodes of the Godard celebration. This was not an occasion designed for the world stage with the international press in attendance and American money changing hands: this was an event *de chez nous*. If the Godard was critically prestigious, the Lefebvre was extraordinarily intimate. If the Godard produced tears of exhaustion, the Lefebvre brought on tears of gratitude and appreciation. No wonder that with all this emotional stretching, I was becoming increasingly strung out.

But that wasn't all. I had also agreed with Geraldine Sherman to deliver four hours of radio on the state of theatrical funding. "You can't refuse me," she had said. "It's your field." Working with Gordon Vogt, a dear friend who had been one of my students at Queen's, I had already begun to collect material. Now we had to scramble to get ready for a play-date in March.

Gord had been the drama critic for CBC's "Stereo Morning" in the days when Terry Campbell hosted it and, along with scraps of music, it offered mini reviews of the arts. Gord was already suffering from the sliver of cancer in his brain that was soon to kill him. He had wonderful insights and was one of the world's most beautiful people; but he was having trouble organizing his ideas, in finding a shape appropriate for what he wanted to say.

We had to prepare the shows. I summoned him to Ottawa. I had set up an editing table so we could finalize the programs.

It was a dramatic weekend. Fuelled by alcohol and nervous determination, I sat at the table, my tape-recorder on one side and my typewriter on the other, while Gord selected bits of tape and talked about how they might be used. From his "might" came my "must" and within two days we had our shows.

Up in Toronto the following week, in studio with Geraldine and Lorne Tulk—the technical wizard who, among other things, had overseen all the Glenn Gould radio documentaries—Gord had trouble speaking his own scripts. This was astonishing. He had a beautiful voice and had had some experience as a professional actor. None of us realized, Gord himself included, just how sick he was. Within a year he would be dead.

The shows were very different from other things I had done. Far more informational, they cautioned listeners about the dangers lurking for Canadian theatre if it went the way of Canadian film, which at that time had been seriously deformed by tax write-off schemes. Indeed, the shows anticipated the "touristization" of theatre culture in Toronto and the growing dominance of the lavish "franchise" shows like *Phantom of the Opera* and *Les Misérables*.

No-one seemed to notice. By the late nineteen-seventies, both public policy and private initiative were increasingly committed to developing more industrial than cultural strategies for the arts. The tycoons had learned to lobby and the artists weren't being heard. "Canadian Theatre on the Brink—Lessons from the Canadian Cinema" was prepared and broadcast but it disappeared without a trace.

By that time, working with the full co-operation of Sam Kula at the National Film Archives in Ottawa, my colleague Zuzana Pick and myself were also in the throes of organizing a full-scale retrospective of the achievements of Québécois cinema, complete with simultaneous translation and voice-over commentaries for a number of key films that had never been subtitled. The idea was to present the québécois achievement to English-speaking academics. The Film Studies Association of Canada had only just got started and it was our desire to invite our Québécois colleagues into our group, to make them feel at home.

Although it was a great celebration, culturally it was a

disaster. Virtually no Anglophones appeared. While the Québécois were there in substantial numbers and had a good time, all of us getting drunk in my garden on the last day of the event, the result of that reunion was that the Québécois decided to form their own association.

Although there is still a handful of Francophones that attends our annual conferences and an even smaller handful of Anglophones that attends theirs, basically—like the two divisions within Radio Canada and the CBC—we now go our separate ways, drawing upon different traditions and focusing on diverse concerns.

After that conference, I set out for the Maritimes in my by-now even rustier Volkswagen. I had agreed to teach a summer school on Canadian film for the Department of Education at Dalhousie University. Feeling atavistically drawn to the east, I was looking forward to it. I thought I might heal. The strain of the year had brought my live-in relationship in Ottawa to an end and by a strange set of circumstances, I had arranged with my old friend and divorce companion from Kingston to travel about together for a few days after the summer school, just to see if we got on.

We didn't. So once again, I lost two women in one year! After a drunken trip to Newfoundland, I returned to Ottawa for my first Carleton sabbatical where I sat in my rocking-chair in my now half-empty house with a bottle of scotch in my hand and I wept and howled and saw virtually no-one. The CFI had all but collapsed and my former colleagues and friends had gone.

Those winter months are a blur. As spring came around, however, I rallied and flew off to England. The gentle softness of the country and the unquestioning acceptance of my English friends began to restore me. Even the madness of the Falkland war filled me with joy.

I first heard about it on the BBC. Having described the

Argentine seizure, in that reserved British way the announcer continued: "It is feared the inhabitants of the islands will have to learn Spanish. They may even have to drive on the right-hand side of the road."

I couldn't believe it. Irony on the national news! Something in the British sense of perspective began to restore my own. I felt able to return home.

During my years in Toronto and my first two years in Ottawa, I had lost the habit of reflective thought. That is nonsense, on one level, since I was engaged in all those activities and wrote those two books. Yet on another, it was as if I were working from past ideas: I was so busy producing I had no time to absorb. I was using myself up.

My cultural work felt increasingly irrelevant. I had become so evangelical that everyone thought I was crazy. Perhaps I was; but I saw the characteristics of the Canada I had returned to being systematically dismantled and no-one in authority seemed to care.

It wasn't "hip" to care. We were entering a period of the pervasively cool, of the stylish stance, of the detached and indifferent attitude. We were entering the world in which we now live—a world of the increasing relativism of all values except the unchallengeable value of conspicuous consumption.

The trouble with nationalism in the nineteen-eighties was that there was no longer any concept of Canada that could mobilize itself sufficiently to speak for the country as a whole. Except in Quebec, the nineteenth-century belief in a cultur-ally homogenous nation state had become *passé* and nothing new had taken its place. That is where we are today.

My last major project for the Toronto film festival occurred in 1984. The previous year, I had organized a mini-retrospective of Canadian documentary, placing Canadian films themati-cally within the context of world achievement. It was a wonderful retrospective but it got lost within the totality of the festival. As it was given inadequate publicity, it got an inadequate audience. If the small group of us who attended all had a good time, it was really just Peter Harcourt and his filmmaking friends.

The whole thrust of the festival was changing. It was on its way to becoming one of the most prestigiously comprehensive festivals in the world. The kind of personalized, "signature" programming that I had done in the past was becoming impossible. However, partly owing to the fiasco of the documentary event, Wayne Clarkson suggested that for the following year we organize a full retrospective, showing everything of value that had ever been made in Canada. "If you occupy half the screens," he explained, "you'll get half the press."

Initially, I had hesitations. Was this going to be a grand sop thrown to the Canadian cinema so that they would never have to deal with it again? Furthermore, I had become involved with a National Film Board production-training project that would keep me in Edmonton for most of the summer. But we decided to go ahead, with me taking much of the credit but with Piers Handling doing most of the work.

The festival arranged for the publication of two books to accompany the event—Peter Morris' *The Film Companion*, and *Take Two*, compiled by Seth Feldman—an anthology of articles already written, including several by myself.

Screening over a hundred films in the course of ten days, the retrospective was an enormous success. People were turned away from almost all screenings. In many cases, new prints had been struck and Québécois films freshly subtitled. After the screening of Don Shebib's *Goin' Down the Road*, the audience hoisted him up on their shoulders and carried him out of the cinema! While audiences had stayed away in droves the previous year from Pierre Perrault's *La bête lumineuse*, they thronged all three screenings of the "Ile aux Coudres" trilogy—*Pour la suite du monde, Le règne du jour*, and *Les voitures d'eau*.

I couldn't believe it. Piers couldn't believe it. Geoff Pevere couldn't believe it. With his cowboys boots on his desk, a packet of Gauloises to hand, his earring sparkling in the sun and an I-told-you-so smile on his face, only Wayne Clarkson believed it. Wayne had already developed a golden touch within the corporate world. Anything he initiates is automatically a success.

Furthermore, it wasn't just a token. The retrospective inaugurated a yearly series of "Perspectives Canada" screenings that, without exception, play to packed houses. The fact that, when the films move from the festival to the commercial screens elsewhere in the city, they seldom last for more than a few weeks demonstrates that, in present-day consumer culture, people are more interested in events than in films. But that is another story.

While offering film courses for the Institute of Canadian Studies at Carleton University, I had been approached a number of times to design a more general cultural seminar. I finally decided to accept the challenge.

I had dipped into this literature in the past, adducing the names of George Grant, Northrop Frye, and Harold Innis when teaching courses in Canadian film. Now, however, I would explore the field more thoroughly. I wanted to see if this intellectual tradition might have laid the foundations for a Canadian culture. I wanted to explore how different people had imagined our country.

Supervising this seminar has been a revelation. First of all, I was astonished at how little I knew. While a cultural activist in good standing, I had only the scrappiest knowledge of our intellectual traditions.

Secondly, the students knew even less. There was no canon of accepted texts. Most students had been exposed to Margaret Atwood's *Survival* but very few to Northrop Frye's writings on Canadian culture, let alone to D.G. Jones, Susan Crean, John Moss, Marcel Rioux, Frank Davey or Robin Mathews. Historians such as Donald Creighton were not known at all;

and as for R. Murray Schafer's work on musical soundscapes or Barry Lord's contestational re-ordering of Canadian painting: these texts were known, if at all, only if there were musicians or art historians in the group. With his bumper-sticker formulations, Marshall McLuhan was accepted as a pop guru; and while everyone had *heard* of him, no-one had *read* Harold Innis.

Canada must be the only country in the world that fails to put its own achievement at the centre of its educational system. This failure may in large part explain our traditional niceness; but it also explains why, as a distinct entity, we are being eroded away.

Attempting to recover the cultural traditions that have helped form the Canadian sensibility has been immensely rewarding but ultimately disheartening. It has been rewarding because, through an exploration of the work of the Wise White Males of Canadian thought, I have come to recognize aspects of myself. It has been disheartening, however, because endlessly remedial. These traditions constitute a series of educational priorities that have been ignored and which by now are frozen in the past.

Even the way that Canada has been imagined is archaic. If Innis' study of the fur trade helped Donald Crieghton to develop the Laurentian theory of Canadian history, which in turn gave Northrop Frye some of his most resounding metaphors for the territorial feel of Canada as a nation, these theories are all dependent on antiquated technologies.

By explaining life in terms of resource commodities—of fish and fur and lumber and coal—and in terms of transportation—of boats over water and railways over land—Innis developed a paradigm for cultural thinking that is distinctively Canadian but which is also distinctly deterministic. Furthermore, by relating issues of national space to specific technologies, his thought has helped to unravel our sense of nation with the development of new, paranational technologies. Nevertheless, certain ideas remain.

Marcel Rioux has suggested that, while Europeans are people of time, North Americans are people of space. And yet, Innis' insights concerning the necessary balance between time-biased and space-biased technologies of communication provide a useful template for an understanding of Canada. After all, it was by refusing the American War of Independence that we declared our commitment to historical continuity; and our sense of space has always had more to do with development than with conquest. These temporal and spatial metaphors have affected our collective imagination, allowing us to achieve something like a Canadian myth.

If Americans have mythologized the frontier, Canadians have mythologized the St. Lawrence River. Québécois films from *Pour la suite du monde* to *Le vieux pays où Rimbaud est mort* have invited the St. Lawrence to stand for their country; while in *The Commercial Empire of the St. Lawrence*, Donald Creighton has written about our mighty river with a rhetorical power worthy of Walt Whitman.

> It was the one great river which led from the eastern shore into the heart of the continent. It possessed a geographical monopoly; and it shouted its uniqueness to adventurers. The river meant mobility and distance; it invited journeyings; it promised immense expanses, unfolding, flowing away into remote and changing horizons. The whole west, with all its riches, was the dominion of the river. To the unfettered and ambitious, it offered a pathway to the central mysteries of the continent ...

Whatever the value of such writing as history, as potential mythology it is enormously effective. Think too of that famous passage from *The Bush Garden* by Northrop Frye, describing the geographical differences between Canada and the United States:

... Canada has, for all practical purposes, no Atlantic seaboard. The traveller from Europe edges into it like a tiny Jonah entering an inconceivably large whale, slipping past the Straits of Belle Isle into the Gulf of St. Lawrence, where five Canadian provinces surround him, for the most part invisible. Then he goes up the St. Lawrence and the inhabited country comes into view, mainly a French-speaking country, with its own cultural traditions. To enter the United States is a matter of crossing an ocean; to enter Canada is a matter of being silently swallowed by an alien continent.

The sense of Canada as a space that engulfs one is central to the myth of survival in Canadian culture. True or not, such master images are necessary to galvanize the collective imagination, to make possible the sense of nation as an imagined community.

But these texts are not known; and our collective ignorance of them provides the context for George Grant's lament about the "irrelevance" of Canada. In his opposition to technology and to the idea of time as progress, he sees the American emphasis on efficiency as the great culprit in the erosion of the values of Canadian life.

Collectively, the voices of these fine thinkers constitute what I have called "The Lonely Discourse" in Canadian thought. This discourse might have helped preserve Canada as a cultural entity had it been widely disseminated and thoroughly discussed. Even at the time of utterance, however, there was a feeling in the voices of these men that they would never be adequately listened to or effectively understood.

Possibly they realized that they were extolling the values of a vanishing culture—and not just the culture of Canada but also the culture of male privilege. Rooted in the achievements of the European past, even more than Matthew Arnold idolizing the ancient Greeks, they didn't see too clearly what was happening around them.

Lamenting in their different ways the loss of an oral tradition, they lacked the foresight to recognize in the repressed ghettoes of aboriginal peoples another, *potentially* more relevant oral tradition that might have played an energizing role in the development of Canada if the franco/anglo conquerors had ever been able adequately to acknowledge it.

Intimations of the cost of this inability are most clearly present in the writings of George Grant. In an essay published in *Technology and Empire*, Grant acknowledges the Canadian fact of genocide and the consequent annihilation of the gods indigenous to our land.

> That conquering relation to place has left its mark within us. When we go into the Rockies we may have the sense that gods are there. But if so, they cannot manifest themselves to us as ours. They are the gods of another race, and we cannot know them because of what we are, and what we did. There can be nothing immemorial for us except the environment as object.

This passage, however, is as much sentimental as analytical. Grant must have recognized that the holy projections of our aboriginal peoples would have been without written language, without any sense of evolving time, and certainly without any interest in technologies of progress. They could have been far more nurturing to the collective Canadian consciousness than Grant's beloved Greeks or punitive Christians. It is one of the enormous limitations of this Lonely Discourse, restorative though it can be, that it couldn't incorporate the spiritual inheritance of our land.

If this tradition of philosophical reflection lives on today, it is to be found with most authority in the work of Bruce Elder. More than anyone I know, his whole manner radiates intensity and intelligence. While we disagree about many things concerning art and culture and about their relationship to social life, even the most casual conversation with Bruce challenges my mind for months at a time. In his book, *Image and Identity*, he celebrates the experimental films of Michael Snow for descending directly from the Canadian philosophical tradition. I want to suggest a similar lineage for the work of R. Bruce Elder.

Although a prolific writer, Elder constructs his most complex philosophical statements within his films. Refusing traditional narrative and conventional representation, in extended cinematic poems such as *Lamentations* and *Consolations*, Elder further explores the Jeremiah tradition of George Grant, lamenting the values now vanished from a spiritually arid world.

More directly than Grant, Elder confronts the inheritance of native spirituality. But for Elder, it is too late. Toward the end of *Lamentations*, he takes us into the space of aboriginal worlds, first in Mexico and then in Peru. The native celebrations are represented as festival events for tourists. The spiritual essence of their religious ceremonies has been commercialized and deformed.

While Elder's work is difficult—indeed, as Bruce himself can be—my ongoing friendship with him has been intellectually the most challenging that I have ever had in my life.

It is one of my deep regrets, however, that I never met George Grant. Since he too liked his scotch, we might have got on together. From everything I have heard about him, his force was in his teaching. Like F.R. Leavis who was also an exponent of an oral tradition, Grant was probably more himself in speech than in writing. His books seem mere traces of what must have been the full power of the man.

I did encounter Northrop Frye, however, on a number of occasions; and one morning we had breakfast together. We were both staying at the Château Versailles in Montreal. He was working on his second book on the Bible and, to my surprise, was reading Elder's *Image and Identity*. "Well, that's also theology," I suggested. Frye agreed. His interest in Elder confirmed my sense that there is indeed a Great Tradition in Canadian thought. Although not part of our everyday experience, it is there when we seek it out.

If our cinema has been an invisible cinema, as I have often suggested—a cinema that exists but that remains unseen; our intellectual culture has been an inaudible culture—a culture that exists but that has not been heard. Investigating these matters, one works like an archaeologist, burrowing amongst the remnants of a past civilization that, on examination, one recognizes as one's own.

Thinking about the places I have been, the things I have done and the thoughts I have had, I am confronted, finally, with a situation impossible to resolve. There are too many variables, too few continuities. Even the continuity of self is increasingly elusive.

If the self is a social construct, as societies shift and change the self too lurches about. Such continuities as the world allows are related to family, to social position and to professional acclaim. When these too shift, a settled sense of self becomes increasingly obscure.

I have always lived my life through other people. I have needed their approval. I have had to live for something beyond myself, to animate my existence and vitalize my spirit.

This dependency began, of course, with my sister; and it has continued to make me imaginatively dependent upon women. My quests have always been less sensual than psychological. I would even say spiritual, except that that word has surrendered much of its currency within the contemporary world. Nowadays, *Beatrice* would be a feminist.

This psychic dependency also explains my life in film. More immediately than music or literature, films create an imaginary world, a world of unspecified fantasy and desire. Dramatizing personal conundrums, they have evoked cultural situations in which I could immerse myself, swimming more securely within their currents than I could within the whirlpools of my own life.

When still married with my children about me, I felt the critical life a complement to my actual life; but looking back on things, I fear that the people closest to me may have felt me at a distance, as if something were missing in some way.

This too goes back to childhood—to the absence of myself in my own memories and to the curse of my analytical cast of mind. As age has crept up on me and solitude has become increasingly my companion, I feel more and more detached even from those few friends and colleagues who still find time for me.

The nineteen-nineties are not a social age and Ottawa is the least social space in which I have ever lived. When I first arrived here, I thought Ottawans were friendly. Later I realized they are only polite. The university, too, is polite. Unionized in all of its relationships, there are no passions anywhere, no sense of collective commitments. If an enriching education must involve both practical and theoretical elements, if it must stimulate the imagination as much as it disciplines the mind, at Carleton University in the nineteen-nineties, the first part of this twin objective has been all but totally ignored.

In England in the nineteen-sixties, there was a cultural community. There were people who cared. In Canada in the nineteen-nineties, although there is a lot of informed chit-chat about culture, especially on the CBC, there is no energizing politics. Such constituencies as now exist are too dispersed. The older traditions seem vestigial and the new ones are still struggling to emerge.

While I enjoy plunking out bits of Bach and Bartók on my digital piano, the one privilege that remains in my life springs from my continued access to young people. Although the cultural gap between my students and myself gets wider every year, the energy of their interests continues to give me hope.

"Life's a casting off, Willie," said his wife to Willy Loman in *Death of a Salesman* back in 1949. It has always amazed me how isolated lines from books and plays have claimed a prophetic space in my memory. I was no more than a teenager when I first heard that line at the Royal Alexandra theatre in Toronto; yet even then I seemed to know what it meant.

As the world cascades with greater and greater acceleration toward a culture of conspicuous consumption, there is less and less continuity. Wisdom is invalidated. Memory becomes nostalgia. Age less embodies insights than encrusted irrelevancies. This *is* no country for old men.

Since my early family situation failed to provide a strong sense of self, my pursuit of knowledge has been an attempt to re-invent myself. For a while it worked. My role in developing a film culture both in Great Britain and in Canada simulated a sense of self. But once that culture is established, the self slips into history. One is left within an existential void.

Finally, however, these problems are more than personal. They wouldn't be worth contemplating if not symptomatic of a larger cultural situation.

In his various examinations of the sources of the self, in *Reconciling the Solitudes* directly addressing the Canadian situation, philosopher Charles Taylor has written about the need for a "horizon of meaning" to provide stability and identity, as a means of reciprocral recognition within any given cultural space.

> ...what is peculiar to a human subject is the ability to ask and answer questions about what really matters, what is of the highest value, what is truly significant, what is most moving, most beautiful, and so on. The conception of identity is the view that outside the horizon provided by some master value or some allegiance or some community membership, I would be crucially crippled,

would become unable to ask and answer these questions effectively, and would thus be unable to function as a full human subject.

It is this inability to function as a full human subject that most insistently speaks to me. It is as much cultural as personal.

We live now in a world of an increasing spiritual emptiness. Although not without its excitements, the entertainment culture of the United States is the most trivializing the world has ever seen. Far more damaging than the atrocities of Adolph Hitler are the achievements of Walt Disney. He has altered the sensibilities of an entire world with its consent. The inescapable "cuteness" of all entertainment for children now seems without redress. Brought up within the falsifications of the Disneyan imagination, the young are denied access to the mysteries of the world. They are held within what Timothy Findley has called a culture of "commercialized immaturity." Especially in North America, Disneythink exists unchallenged.

In such a situation, I have come to understand why thoughtful Americans like Ezra Pound and T.S. Eliot adopted the politics they did. As Americans, they could see the trivializing future of American democracy—a fate foreseen long before by Alexis de Tocqueville. They could also see in Europe the cultural advantages of oligarchic control. Fearing the future, they wanted to preserve the past—to slow down the great egalitarian American adventure. In gentler ways this has been the project of thoughtful Canadians like George Grant and Northrop Frye as it is today for Bruce Elder.

These consolations are not available to me. Although imaginatively nourished by this tradition, I have come to refuse it. It is too tied to the past. The demographics of the world are changing; and while it is sometimes frightening just what values will emerge from the seismic shifts occurring within our established cultures, I believe that, ultimately, they will be regenerative.

The foreign students I know, especially those from Eastern Europe and from Asia and Africa, are dedicated in ways that I find wonderful to behold. I rarely find a comparable passion among young North Americans. Disneythink has made them cynical. They have too many material things and too few inner resources. With the Europeans and the Africans, however, at least those who come to Canada, it is the other way round.

These young new Canadians give me hope. If I am particularly aware of the limitations both of myself and my culture, it is because such privileges as I acquired I wasn't really born to. They didn't fully take. Not only in my personal but in my cultural life, I have been too randomly promiscuous. I have had to confront the relativity of so many things.

And yet, values are not relative. Only their individual manifestations. There has been no culture at any time in the history of the world that has not been rooted in some form of belief system. Whatever social injustices these belief systems have entailed, they have allowed the cultures to flourish and have bestowed upon them an enduring dignity. They have engendered a sense of wonder.

The ascendant North American culture of distractive entertainment robs us of dignity. It invalidates wonder. Whatever we now know about the limited resources of the world, however, this consumptive culture cannot continue. Something else will take its place.

During an extended television conversation with Melvyn Bragg a few years ago, Francis Bacon declared his unshakable optimism. In spite of all the pain of life, its ugliness and desperation, he remained optimistic. "Optimistic—about nothing," was the way he put it. I believe it was the life force within him that sustained that faith.

In spite of everything, we live in privileged times. We know so much more about the world than did our ancestors.

We have insights that could change things—and this time, for the better. Young people today are far less bound by the assumptions of their inherited cultures, far more open to the voices of alternative cultures—aboriginal cultures, feminine cultures, ecological cultures. While diminished by Disneythink, they have not been destroyed. If they can find the will, they have the energy to transform the world.

In this way, I too am optimistic about nothing. I believe that, as in the past, the future lies ahead.